Niklas Brunius

Göran O Eriksson

Rolf Rembe

Swedish Theatre

THE SWEDISH INSTITUTE FOR CULTURAL

RELATIONS WITH FOREIGN COUNTRIES

TRANSLATED BY KEITH BRADFIELD

CONTENTS

A Visitor's Impressions

An introduction by Martin Esslin

It would be presumption, for someone who has only paid a few brief visits to Sweden, to go beyond a few fleeting impressions of the Swedish theatre —

— the lovely eighteenth century theatre at Drottningholm, miraculously preserved in the exact state in which it fell into a long hibernation of oblivion after the death of King Gustaf III in 1792, to be rediscovered almost by chance in 1921, and now restored to its former glory, with backdrops and machinery intact —

— or the exuberance of a young company at the Pistol-teatern who concluded a performance excitingly compounded of jazz session, avant-garde film show and "Happening" by attacking the masonry of the little old cinema where they were playing with sledge-hammers in a veritable orgy of destruction. (They explained to me later that they had been given a grant to rebuild the place and that it was therefore both convenient and economical to include some demolition in their show!) —

— or the assurance and quiet technical mastery of Alf Sjöberg's production of Brecht's *Mother Courage* at the Royal Dramatic Theatre, the Dramaten, a performance which could stand comparison with that of the Berliner Ensemble without any fear of being eclipsed and was mercifully free from the besetting sin of most attempts to produce the play, an excessive zeal to copy Brecht's own model —

— or Strindberg's *To Damascus* at the Stockholm City Theatre, all three parts in one evening, brilliantly foreshortened by the use of projected backgrounds which made the scenes merge into each other as in a dream, in a play which is indeed a terrible, tormented, tragic dream —

— or Ingmar Bergman's production of Goethe's *Urfaust* with the company of the Malmö City Theatre with Toivo Pawlo as Faust and Ulf Palme as Mephistopheles, simple, intense and immensely powerful —

What is the special quality that emerges from all these fleeting and disjointed impressions?

It is, I feel, a combination of exuberance, emotional intensity and a delight in laughter, colour and movement on the one hand, with a deep underlying *earnestness;* earnestness not in the sense of seriousness or pedantry, but earnestness as a determination to devote to an art form which is deeply loved and regarded as deeply important the highest degree of skill and affectionate care of which all concerned are capable. There is nothing slapdash here, nothing dilettantish or half-hearted . . . Is it that in a country with a cold climate and long dark winters the pursuit of colour and light, the quest for the power of magical transformations is a real necessity, a basic human need which must be satisfied? I don't think that I am in a position to answer that question. I can merely pose it.

What I can say is that in my view — and I have devoted much time to the study of the organization of theatre in a variety of different countries — the Swedish theatre is a real model of rationality, of an enlightened cultural policy. For someone who is used to the organization of the theatre as we have it in the English-speaking countries, the Swedish system (which is on the lines of what is normal in Germany, Central and Eastern Europe, but in many ways more enlightened) must be a revelation: the commercial system of single productions financed ad hoc by speculative "backers" does not exist. Even private theatres have permanent companies with long-term contracts for the actors. And even private theatres sometimes receive financial aid from the state and the municipalities. And the fully subsidized state and municipal theatres receive grants far above the level of even those of the Arts Council in Britain. It is not merely that the level of subsidies it receives from the state and municipal bodies must appear lavish to an observer from a country like Britain where state support of the arts, the conception of art as an amenity to which the community has a right, has only just begun to make an impact; it is rather the way in which a method has been found to apply this patronage without political interference or censorship on the one hand, without an inhibition of genuine creative talents and new initiatives on the other. Not only the famous and long-established institutions like the Dramaten receive subsidies, they are also available to young avant-gardists like the splendid young team at the Pistolteatern, provided that they can show by their own initiative and self-sacrificing devotion to their ideas that they can make good use of the financial help available.

In some countries where the theatre receives generous support from the state, but where this support entails close supervision by a bureaucracy and imposes a rigid pattern, the system of subsidies results in a complacent, lifeless, lazy atmosphere in the theatre. In Sweden there is little sign of any such phenomenon. Those responsible for running the theatre in Sweden seem to me to make a splendid use of the freedom they enjoy: the catholicity of the repertoire is astonishing. Often important English or American plays get onto the stage in Sweden before they even reach a performance in their original language. It is no accident that Eugene O'Neill reserved the first performances of his posthumous right to the Royal Dramatic Theatre in Stockholm. Wherever a new and important, or even merely interesting, dramatist appears in Western, but also in Eastern Europe, he is certain to be spotted by the eagle eyes of Swedish theatre people. Nor is there any sign of complacency among actors, directors or designers. Partly, no doubt, this is due to the high level of professional education Swedish theatre people receive, their intelligence and integrity; partly, I think, it is due to the stimulus of a really interested public opinion, which, moreover, in a country with so high a standard of living where trips abroad are available to all, is constantly stimulated by the public's ability to compare with standards abroad; but mainly, I am convinced, the absence of complacency and stagnation is due to the presence of directors like Bergman, Sjöberg or Sundström, who are real artists and at the same time inspiring leaders of their fellow artists. Good theatre, in the last resort, is the product of collective action by a team; and teams must be formed, forged and held together by great personalities. The Swedish theatre is fortunate in possessing a relatively large number of such directors. And, by giving chances to young people who show the potential for such leadership, the Swedish system of public support provides an insurance against any danger that the supply of great artistic personalities might cease. It is an admirable system which opens up splendid prospects for the future of the Swedish theatre.

NIKLAS BRUNIUS

The Swedish Theatre

The Swedish theatre is an important chapter in our country's cultural history. Its traditions are long, and its present organization has provided a model for experiments abroad. The roots of our modern Swedish theatre lie in the 18th century theatre of Gustaf III. The latter form of theatre was by no means unique — court theatres existed at that time throughout Europe — but Gustaf III opened the doors of his theatre to the burghers of Stockholm, who had previously had to content themselves with more sporadic performances. He created also a Swedish theatre in the sense that the actors spoke Swedish. Previously, the court theatre had performed almost exclusively in French. Gustaf III realized, however, that if he was to make theatre-goers (and royal fellow-travellers) of the general public, he must first clear the ground by introducing opera. He succeeded in the course of a single year in giving a magnificent start to Swedish opera, with a succession of new works on patriotic and royalistic themes. He also succeeded to some extent in raising the social status of the theatre.

In 1788, he opened the Royal Dramatic Theatre, the sole purpose of which he declared to be the performance of Swedish drama. Within a year or two, the impossibility of this was realized and the repertory of Swedish theatre began to be international. The policy of a mixed repertory was continued during the 19th century. In the 20th century, American, English and French plays in particular have been produced. Major plays are now often produced simul-

Jack, or The Submission by Eugène Ionesco. Directed by Per Åhlin. Theatre 23, 1965.

taneously at theatres throughout the country. This alignment with foreign drama has had no counterpart in the major theatre-producing countries, such as France and England, even if the past ten years have seen a radical change in this respect: a more extrovert repertory, with frequent exchanges of guest performances, is precisely what characterizes current development in Paris and London.

Gustaf III's court theatre, which shortly became a national stage, is the prototype also of the Swedish theatre's organization. Private theatres in Sweden have always been of relatively minor importance: occasional private companies, touring provincial players and short-lived enterprises in Stockholm have been exceptions to prove the rule. Swedish theatre is thus the national stage: the Royal Dra-

The Sport of My Mad Mother by Ann Jelicoe. Directed by Johan Bergenstråhle. Here Maud Hansson and Jan Bergquist. Stockholm City Theatre, 1966.

matic Theatre and the municipal theatres in the provinces. (See map on page 14.) All these companies are subsidized: the Dramatic Theatre, for instance, received in 1967—68 SKr[1] 9,695,000 (approx. US $ 1,874,275) from the state.

These grants suffice to maintain a permanent company and present a number of artistically high-standing productions. The attendance is of minor importance, although it naturally influences discussions between the governing board and the theatre manager. The latter has entirely free hands in his choice of repertory. The board, of course, can voice its opinions but the decision on all artistic matters rests with the manager. Political pressure from the government or local council is unknown.

[1] £ 1 = SKr 14.45, $ 1 = SKr 5.17

Cities with state-supported theatres.

The Royal Dramatic Theatre

The Royal Dramatic Theatre is a share company with privately owned shares. Its manager is chosen by the King in Council, as is its board. The board and theatre manager are jointly responsible for finances, while the manager alone chooses productions and provides the artistic leadership. To assist him he has a council (created in 1963) consisting of five actors chosen by their colleagues. These have no rights of decision but function as an advisory body in, above all, casting. The Dramatic Theatre has seven permanently employed directors and about seventy actors. Some fifteen—twenty new productions are presented every year on two stages (800 and 350 seats). At present, it is possible to retain a successful production in the repertory for about one year. This was the case, for instance, with Brecht's *Mother Courage and Her Children* which was performed 80 times.

Municipal theatres

The most influential of the municipal theatres has been that in Gothenburg (Göteborg). This originated in the Lorensberg Theatre formed in 1918 and supported by the wealthy Gothenburg *bourgeoisie*. Modernists Knut Ström and Per Lindberg experimented here for some years along German lines, producing e.g. Shakespeare, Strindberg and modern drama. The break with the Parisian traditions of the Swedish theatre was made here without any great fuss. In the mid-1930s Gothenburg was given a new stage, to which the Lorensberg company was mowed. This theatre, with its stage and machinery designed by Knut Ström, is still — thirty years later — one of the most modern in Europe. It was in the Gothenburg City Theatre that the idea of a municipal theatre was first completely realized. The great interest of the 1930s in a "folk theatre", a giant stage providing committed drama to the masses, meant seeking new categories of audience. A system of regular subscriptions was introduced on the pattern of the German *Volksbühne*. The Gothenburg City Theatre followed its radical policy throughout the Second World War by producing plays that were unperformable on the national stage of a neutral country. Its manager, Torsten Hammarén, showed here the same uncompromising resistance to Nazism as Torgny Segerstedt, editor of Gothenburg's *Handels- och Sjöfartstidning*. The theatre had also an outstanding company, including Elsa Widborg, Sven Milliander and Kolbjörn Knudsen.

The Malmö City Theatre is our best example of a "folk theatre" in Per Lindberg's sense of the term. Lindberg played an invaluable part in the preparatory work for this theatre, but died before it was completed. The main stage of the Malmö City Theatre is enormous: the auditorium is in the form of an amphitheatre, and the stage, with its gigantically long proscenium, is very difficult to use. The only producer who has really succeeded in mastering its vast surfaces is naturally enough Ingmar Bergman, who staged several of his most famous productions there between 1953 and 1960.

The northern part of Sweden has been very much of an undeveloped area, so far as the theatre is concerned. In the autumn of 1967 a regional theatre was opened in Luleå. Shamefully, only about one-third of Sweden has so far had access to a permanent theatre.

As an example of the finances and organization of the municipal theatres, we can take the Gothenburg City Theatre. This received SKr 2,214,000 from the local council, and SKr 2,376,000 from the state in 1966–67. Its organization differs very little from that of the Royal Dramatic Theatre, although its resources are smaller: 48 actors and 4 directors in 1966–67. We can note also that the boards of the munic-

Uncle Vanya by Anton Chekhov. Directed by Ulf Palme. Sophia Alexandrovna — Bibi Andersson, Marina — Dagmar Bentzen. Uppsala City Theatre, 1962.

ipal theatres have greater powers than that of the Dramatic Theatre.

The National Touring Theatre

An organization that has carried drama from Stockholm to the provinces, is the National Touring Theatre, which has been active since the early 1930s. The idea of a touring theatre was naturally not new in Sweden, but the concept of a "folk theatre" gave it increased impetus. This state-subsidized organization sends out a number of plays on tour at the same time. The difficulties of such a system are obvious. Few of the stages available are technically adequate; the acting space and acoustics vary enormously; and actors, in spite of the good wages, are unwilling in the long run to live like nomads. Since 1966, the National Touring Theatre has been incorporated with another touring theatre, the Swedish Theatre, and is at present being modernized to meet current standards of good theatre.

Dramatists

August Strindberg is still the only Swedish dramatist of outstanding importance. During his lifetime, Strindberg had difficulty in placing his plays on the Swedish market. But, however blasphemous and disgusting they were considered at the time, Strindberg's dramas have since 1910 been a source from which Swedish playwrights have drunk their fill. In the long run, this has had a somewhat negative effect: but we have been unable to get round him, his attitude to life haunts us; stylistic conceits have been directly transferred from Strindberg to the younger generation. If Strindberg's dream play technique has exercised a great influence on our dramatists, it is his naturalistic tragedies that have been most beloved of the theatres, resulting in a style of acting in the Swedish theatre, particularly at the Dramatic Theatre, that is "psychologizing" and naturalistic to a

Arturo Ui by Bertolt Brecht. Directed by Peter Palitzsch. Dogs-
borough — Åke Grönberg, Arturo Ui — Toivo Pawlo. Stockholm
City Theatre, 1966.

marked degree. The psychological motives for every action
are legion; the complicated character is assigned a higher
value than the simple and straightforward; internal conflicts
and doubts attract greater interest than conflicts between
political or religious groups. Strindberg, like Wagner, has
inspired his successors to tread closely in his footsteps, and
what they have produced are for the most part copies: very
few have been able to employ Strindberg's experiences in
a new way.

   One of those who had this ability was Nobel prize win-
ner Pär Lagerkvist in the expressionistic dramas of his
youth. He could play out forces dramatically against each

19

Good Old Pearl by Karl Erik Johansson i Backe. Directed by Per-Axel Branner. Here Sigge Fischer and Rut Cronström. National Touring Theatre, 1965.

other, but came unfortunately close to pure abstraction: his concern for clarity led sometimes to dryness. Lagerkvist is even so one of the most important of expressionistic playwrights. His plays are rare guests to the stage, but the quality of such dramatic works as *The Secret of Heaven* and *The Hour of Trial* will surely lead to a renewed interest in their production.

Hjalmar Bergman, Pär Lagerkvist's contemporary, has been far more successful in winning the ear of the general public. His plays have nothing of Lagerkvist's severity of form, although there are naturally exceptions. His three *Marionette Plays,* of which the masterpiece *Mr. Sleeman Is Coming* is best known, resemble in many ways Strindberg's chamber plays, but his really popular works are entirely conventional in form. *The Swedenhielms,* his comedy of a Swedish genius, is a run-of-the-mill work that could have been written by any skilled French or English dramatist, and Bergman's most popular plays, *His Grace's Last Will* and *God's Orchid* are admittedly very amusing, but stereotyped and thinned-down versions of his novels with the same titles.

Playwrights of the 1930s

The 1930s saw a cultural revolution in Sweden. The workers began to write their own literature. A fairly large group of young writers came from the working classes, and both peasant plays and dramas of the class struggle had their champions. Rudolf Värnlund was a young writer who showed great promise as a playwright. He had the ability to choose subjects of basic importance and handle them forcefully and persuasively. What he lacked was the patience to work over the uneven sketches that his dramas have remained. Värnlund claimed that he could afford neither the time nor the money to polish his work, and this seems unfortunately to have been true. He earned his living from hack-work over and above his serious writing. Värnlund is the least known of important Swedish dramatists, but his engagement in external events and his refusal to over-psychologize make him in several ways a healthier acquaintance than many other Swedish writers. His sweeping lines, his glorious rhythm, the freshness of his sketches are naturally also an inheritance from Strindberg, but from a neglected part of Strindberg's work that should now be made the core of our Strindbergian repertory — the historical plays.

Apart from Hjalmar Bergman, Vilhelm Moberg is the only playwright really to have won the heart of the Swedish people. Moberg's peasant dramas are in no way unique — they have numerous counterparts in the other Scandinavian countries — but they possess a compelling force and authenticity, and they are also very well constructed. Moberg has the capacity quite simply to tell a story in a consistently interesting and exciting manner. His attempts to handle the problems of other social classes have failed. Such plays, however, have proved no less dear to the hearts of theatre-goers than his pictures of peasant life. What makes Moberg so enjoyable, even in his less successful works, is the honesty with which he sees himself, and the intensity with which he handles his subject. He contains nothing of artifice or aestheticism. Moberg's latest major play *Your Time on Earth* is a dramatization of the novel by the same name, concentrating on one great theme from the book. The dead can be more alive for us than the living. This play had its première at the Royal Dramatic Theatre in 1967.

Herbert Grevenius belongs to the same generation as Moberg. If Moberg's strength has lain in his portrayals of country people, Grevenius' plays capture with exquisite humour the lives of office workers, the everyday fates of everyday people in the somewhat drab Sweden of the 30s and 40s.

Post-war drama

No major Swedish playwrights have emerged since the war. The curse of Strindberg is still upon us. Several minor talents have emerged: Stig Dagerman, an agonized young writer who had much in common with our expressionists of the 1920s, made a sensational debut with his drama, *Condemned to Death,* before he was hardly come of age, wrote a few more plays, but never really succeeded as a playwright. A couple of his novels, on the other hand, have been successfully filmed. Ingmar Bergman is least known as a dramatist, but was very active in this capacity around 1950. His best known play, however, is of later date: his *Wood Painting* written in 1954 for the Dramatic Academy in Malmö and handling the same subject as his film *The Seventh Seal*. The wastes of northern Sweden, with their inhabitants' agony of soul, their religious and sexual problems, have been portrayed by Björn-Erik Höijer in a number of plays, of which *Isak Juntti Had Many Sons* can be regarded as the most workmanlike. Tore Zetterholm has taken up topical, often international problems and given them a certain dramatic force. Influenced beyond all doubt by Peter Weiss, he showed new potential fields for his writing in *The Women of Shanghai,* 1967. Werner Aspenström has the opposite approach: he often portrays social reality very ironically in the form of unrealistic tales; he is at his best when working in the small format, where his ingenious art of suggestion has achieved triumphs. His latest play *I Have to Go to Berlin* is based on fact, an episode in the life of Isadora Duncan, her love story with the young Russian poet Yesemin, narrated with irony and tenderness.

Erland Josephson, the present head of the Royal Dramatic Theatre, has achieved success with a number of intelligent, well-written plays, the basic virtue of which has been their verbal facility. Most acclaimed has been his bitter comedy *Party Game*. Josephson's latest play *The Last Days of Dr Meyer* treats of an isolated alien in modern Sweden. The most imaginative of the writers who have established themselves in the Swedish theatre is Lars Forssell. His *Sunday Promenade* (1963) was a macabre Swedish idyll from the turn of the century. A great success was his *The Madcap,* i.e. Gustaf IV Adolf, the only Swedish king ever to be deposed. If *Sunday Promenade* was in the style of Hjalmar Bergman, *The Madcap* was more of a Strindbergian chronicle. Forssell is something so unusual as a visionary in the Swedish theatre. Sandro Key-Åberg is a poet, whose dramatic gifts were discovered when the Student Theatre in Stockholm staged some verses from his collection *Figures of Speech*. The result was so successful

Figures of Speech by Sandro Key-Åberg. Directed by Hans Hellberg. Stockholm Student Theatre, 1964.

that it spurred Key-Åberg to further dramatic writing. The dialogues in his *Oh* with its "speaks", took the form of sharp satirical sketches and they handled very serious subjects. The audience was conducted lovingly into the horrors of everyday life, and did not react until they were fast in his trap. *Oh* has most recently been staged in London.

An international dramatist in the true sense, the first after Strindberg, is of course Peter Weiss, whose influence on the development of the theatre cannot yet be foreseen. *Marat-Sade* and *The Investigation* are the most important German dramatic works since Brecht. But since he belongs to another language, Weiss is really outside the scope of this present article.

MOLANDER

A number of great directors have left their mark on the 20th century Swedish theatre. The most important perhaps is Olof Molander, in that he has applied with strict consistency an absolutely unique style of Strindbergian production. He has directed the dream plays and chamber plays in a realistic setting, firmly anchored to the actual places that inspired Strindberg to his later dramas. But by lifting the style a little — not breaking the naturalism but making it unreal — by playing, as it were, six inches above the ground, Molander achieved a surrealistic feeling that revealed a new dimension in many of the later plays. In the 1930s and 1940s, he staged epoch-making productions of *A Dream Play, To Damascus* and *The Ghost Sonata.* The danger with the self-evident authority that radiated from these masterly productions was that it tended to fixate subsequent directors, just as Strindberg himself has paralysed subsequent Swedish dramatists. Ingmar Bergman is the first to admit the restraint he felt when staging *The Ghost Sonata* in Malmö early in the 1950s. The unique thing about Molander is that he, himself, in the autumn of his life, has succeeded in breaking with his own style and creating the embryo of something new in his direction of all three parts of *To Damascus* at the Stockholm City Theatre in 1963. Strindberg was purified in these productions of all realistic details, sole importance being accorded to the words and actors. The simplification that came as such a shock to the audience in Molander's production of Strindberg in 1963, however, was in fact no new vein in this director, whose productions of classical dramas had long been marked by the same severity of style and setting. The most famous of such productions is his *Antigone* (1948), Sophocles' tragedy as a chamber play.

To Damascus by August Strindberg. Directed by Olof Molander, and with Lars Hanson as the Stranger. Royal Dramatic Theatre, 1960.

But even before that, his O'Neill productions of the 1920s, such as *Strange Interlude,* and his production of Euripides' *Medea,* had contained the same tendency towards functionalism. Molander, indeed, is the contemporary of those artists who created the Stockholm Exhibition of 1930, at which functionalism was introduced into Sweden.

LINDBERG

Per Lindberg, a contemporary of Molander's noted his first successes as a director at the Lorensberg Theatre in Gothenburg in collaboration with Knut Ström, whom we have already discussed. Lindberg's strength lay in the freshness, authority and boldness with which he broke the ancient tyranny established by Swedish actors. He turned his back on tradition, but the very force of his direction proved damaging:

a tradition of stylistic acting in the Swedish theatre was abruptly cut off. On the other hand, Lindberg's ability to do the unexpected on the stage, and this not only for the sake of the effect, has surely inspired our younger directors to continued boldness. Lindberg's most famous productions were staged on premises that bore little resemblance to a theatre, namely the Concert Hall in Stockholm. Lindberg had visited Reinhardt in Germany, experienced the latter's *Grosses Schauspielhaus,* and read Romain Rolland's important writings on a popular theatre. His great dream, which he never lived to see realized, was a "folk theatre": the Malmö City Theatre was completed two years after his death. At the Concert Hall he staged above all the classics, from *Agamemnon* in a setting by Carl Milles — who had decorated also the building itself — via Shakespeare's *Antony and Cleopatra* and *Hamlet* to his unique production of *To Damascus III,* with Strindberg's third wife, Harriet Bosse, as the Lady. The predominant feature in Lindberg's productions was the visual effect, awareness of the "play": he made no attempt at "illusion".

BRANNER

Realism, however, had not entirely relinquished its grip. The foremost "listener" among modern Swedish directors is beyond doubt Per-Axel Branner. His great contribution to the Swedish theatre has been the Chekhov productions he produced on his own stage, the Nya Teatern in Stockholm, in the 1940s. Twenty years earlier, the Arts Theatre in Moscow had passed through Sweden on its grand tour of Europe, leaving unforgettable memories that could have only one result — no one in Sweden dared to produce Chekhov. Branner was the first to break this spell and show that the Swedish style of production, with its combination of naturalism and dream play, a style that had

27

emerged thanks to Strindberg's dramas and Molander's production, was very suitable to the Russian temper. Branner repeated his earlier successes during his period as director at the Dramatic Theatre in the 1950s, this time with a highly polished company. He produced *Uncle Vanya* and the *Three Sisters* playing Chekhov home to an international audience in a guest production in Paris at the Théâtre des Nations. The audience could not understand the language, but they were nonetheless gripped by the sensitivity, the musicality of this sharp-eared production. Branner has successfully produced Ibsen in the same manner.

SJÖBERG

The two great directors in the Swedish theatre in 1967 are Alf Sjöberg and Ingmar Bergman, both active at the Royal Dramatic Theatre in Stockholm.

Alf Sjöberg has been employed by this theatre throughout his theatrical career. He started as an actor, playing with outstanding success the main role in Toller's *Hoppla! wir leben* and his early experiences of expressionistic drama have been of decisive importance for his art. This is not to say that he has fastened in the expressionism of the 1920s, but his repeated developments and transformations still find their base note there. Alike in objective, theatrically playful and philosophical drama, it is the violence of movement, the over-charged atmosphere that we feel as important in Alf Sjöberg as a director. He has collaborated also with several of our greatest painters and sculptors, and this has helped him and provided him with a strong foundation of colour and form for his magnificent imagination as a director. Practically all the artists of Sjöberg's generation have worked with him. Men like Sven Erixon, Erik Grate, Stellan Mörner, Sven Erik Skawonius and Lennart Mörk have joined with Sjöberg's richly flowing imagination to offer us

28

our most vital theatrical experiences of the past three decades. Sjöberg has an unusual feeling for movement on the stage (study the way his actors make their entrances in any of his Shakespeare productions), but he creates also the most perfectly balanced groups: his feeling for the beauty and expressiveness of the human body is masterly. The main thing for Sjöberg is the picture: for six months before the rehearsals begin of a Russian play he can sit and study paintings by the great Russian realists. This does not mean that he plagiarizes the pictorial world he studies: he uses art as a springboard from which to give his productions an entirely personal character.

Sjöberg has created outstandingly realistic productions, dominated not by movement but by the internal tensions, by the small relationships between people. Unforgettable are his productions of the *Wild Duck,* the realism of which extended to real herring on the breakfast table in the Ekdals' home, and Tolstoy's *Power of Darkness,* in which hate and goodness, in the shape of the grandmother and grandfather, became at the same time ideas and characters. But Sjöberg's ultimate importance is as a director of Shakespeare and of the Swedish writer Almqvist. His Shakespeare has the same high dignity as Molander's Strindberg: he has made Shakespeare a Swedish classic. His first great successes were noted around 1940, during the war. These were the comedies, in which with the help of Inga Tidblad, leading lady of the Swedish theatre, he shaped these occasionally indigestible plays into masterpieces of lightness, grace and humour. Shakespeare's *Forest of Arden* is associated in Sweden with 19th century Romanticism, the classical translations having been made at that time, but it reflected in Sjöberg's productions a new, modern and perhaps wider revery. Sjöberg has since worked with the tragedies and the chronicles, including *Richard III, Hamlet, Romeo and Juliet* and *Measure for Measure,* but the Shakespeare

King John by William Shakespeare. Directed by Alf Sjöberg. Royal Dramatic Theatre, 1961.

production in which Sjöberg reached furthest in clarity, objectiveness and expressiveness is considered by many to have been his *King John,* 1961. One of Shakespeare's least known plays proved in Sjöberg's production to be one of the most interesting. The war between France and England was presented with an enormous dynamism of collective groupings and movements. That the play has no real main role was only an advantage. The same is true of *Troilus and Cressida,* which Sjöberg staged in the spring of 1967.

A natural development from *King John,* which Sjöberg made dialectical, almost political theatre, came in the three Brecht plays included among his latest productions at the Royal Dramatic Theatre. Quite unexpectedly, he started with *Schweik in the Second World War,* achieving a direct hit. Although this play is regarded as essentially lightweight, it possesses all the components of the great Brechtian plays: wit, entertainment, movement and political discussion, resulting in subsequent thought and a change of attitude. The objective and sarcastic Allan Edwall, with his natural distance, was brilliant in the title role. Sjöberg continued with *Mother Courage and Her Children,* which has been one of the Dramatic Theatre's greatest successes. This was followed in the spring of 1966 by *Puntila.*

The existence of a Swedish dramatist of Strindbergian stature from the early 19th century it was left to Alf Sjöberg to discover. Carl Jonas Love Almqvist is one of the great romantic masters of world literature, and Sjöberg found a perfect material for his scenic art in Almqvist's phantasmagorical and scurrilous writing compounded of novel, poetry and drama. Almqvist possesses the same combination of poetical supersensuality and social pathos that we find in Sjöberg's productions of Shakespeare. Sjöberg's experience from his Shakespearian productions of the 1940s was surely decisive for his ability to interpret the complicated characters of Amorina and Tintomara, which are the core of Almqvist's writing. Tintomara shows the same sexual uncertainty as Viola and Olivia, but it is carried here far beyond the boundaries of playfulness to a seriousness at which her very humanity is questioned. Sjöberg's productions of Almqvist's giant works *Amorina* and *The Queen's Jewel* on the studio stage of the Dramatic Theatre in 1951 and 1956 have perhaps been the younger generation's greatest theatrical experience. It is to be hoped that *Amorina* and *The Queen's Jewel* will soon be translated into the great languages, so that an international public can discover one of the greatest writers in literature — if not in productions by Sjöberg then at least in print.

Alf Sjöberg has shown also a great interest in the new drama: his most important contribution, perhaps, relates to Sartre, whom he was one of the first to produce, with *The Flies* in 1945. Sartre's ties with the naturalistic tradition of theatre have greatly helped the understanding of his plays in

31

Amorina by Carl Jonas Love Almqvist. Directed by Alf Sjöberg and with Anita Björk as Amorina. Left, Hans Strååt. Royal Dramatic Theatre, 1961.

Sweden. Sartre has been approached, in fact, as if he were Strindberg, but Alf Sjöberg had the ability to communicate also his political passion. In Sartre he had to seize on the dialecticalism of the theatre, which he later developed also in his productions of Brecht. Sjöberg's political commitment has, symptomatically enough, influenced also his productions of Ionesco. *The Lesson,* for instance, he concluded with a Nazi salute: the perpetrator of outrage was made a symbol of political violence. In 1965, Sjöberg again made a pioneer contribution when he produced the Polish exile writer Witold Gombrowicz' play *Yvonne, Princess of Burgundy,* forgotten for the past thirty years. Gombrowicz' philosophy has ties with Existentialism, its starting-point being that the situation determines the man. Gombrowicz sees his plays as Shakespearian parodies and they have provided an outstanding score for Sjöberg's unique scenic fan-

Yvonne, Princess of Burgundy by Witold Gombrowicz. Directed by Alf Sjöberg. In the foreground: The King — Sigge Fürst, The Queen — Margaretha Krook, Yvonne — Ulla Sjöblom, Courtier — Ingvar Kjellson. Royal Dramatic Theatre, 1965.

tasy. Gombrowicz' second and still more important play *The Marriage* was staged by Sjöberg in the autumn of 1966. His experience from *Yvonne* carried him here still further into the boldest scenic and mental effects of which the modern theatre is capable. Sjöberg's scenic ability is to concretize the abstract, to give scenic form to what seems almost impossible to realize on the stage, and that in such a way that not only an élite but a wider public could appreciate Gombrowicz' situationist world, in which words and gestures exercise complete power over the characters. Henrik and his father, the two main roles, were played with acuity and heat by Jan-Olof Strandberg and Ernst-Hugo Järegård. One thing is clear enough: Sjöberg's contribution has been important enough to alter the entire development of the Swedish theatre. Working in the Swedish theatre means to a large extent taking sides, for or against Alf Sjöberg's work as a director.

BERGMAN

Ingmar Bergman is one of the best-known personalities of the modern arts: his films are shown throughout the world, he is discussed and compared with Fellini and Buñuel. Relatively little interest has been accorded to his work in the theatre, which is only natural since so few people come into contact with his productions, staged in a single place, for a short period of time and in an obscure language. Nonetheless, Bergman as a man of the theatre is considered in Sweden to stand on the same level as he does as a film creator. He began early as a leader of amateur groups of players, and working in the student theatre. He came to the cinema only later and secondarily. During the last years of the war, he directed a number of plays with professional actors at a committed little theatre where plays were staged that could not otherwise have been produced. Bergman was only 26 years old when he was appointed manager of the Hälsingborg Theatre, and for a couple of years he was given a free hand to do as he pleased. He gathered around him there a young company, produced ten plays a year, lived sparsely and learned a great deal. This irresponsible but merry period, during which he "worked the games out of his system", came to be of great importance when he was employed in 1946 by the strict theatre manager Torsten Hammarén in Gothenburg, and was taught to mind his manners. In Gothenburg he gave us his first great productions, starting with Camus' *Caligula,* which was discussed throughout the town; this was followed by a bloody *Macbeth* and a wonderfully wild and vital production of Valle Inclan's *God's Word in the Country,* which was then entirely unknown in Sweden. His productions were still characterized by a richness and flow of ideas that could sometimes overwhelm the play itself: his inspiration knew no bounds. Even at that time, however, Bergman's eminent ability to make his actors surpass themselves could be discerned. Epoch-making was Ingmar Bergman's fairly long period with the Malmö City Theatre. He was the first to succeed in mastering the giant stage and proscenium of Per Lindberg's "folk theatre", both in his pictorial effects and in his ability to utilize his actors. Bergman likes working with the classics, and his development towards an increasingly clean, "undecorated" style was illustrated by such productions as *Peer Gynt,* with Max von Sydow, *The Misanthrope, Don Juan* and *Faust.* Bergman's love of Swedish found expression in the folk play *The People of Värmland* and a number of outstanding Strindberg productions. On the small studio stage in Malmö he directed Kafka's *The Castle* and Pirandello's *Six Characters in Search of an Author.* He produced also a gentle interpretation of Hjalmar Bergman's *The Legend.* Bergman's great interest in musical theatre has been reflected in a number of productions, including Lehar's *Merry Widow.* His masterpiece was a production at the Royal Opera in Stockholm of Stravinsky's relatively neglected opera *The Rake's Progress.* This work, with its very simple, Spartan décor hovering in the black stage like a pastiche on 18th century theatre, was an enormous popular success, and the aging composer himself expressed great satisfaction at the performance. Following his years in Malmö, Bergman became manager of the Royal Dramatic Theatre in 1963, a post that he left in the spring of 1966.

Our national stage assumed no uniform style during Bergman's period as manager. The rule at this theatre is that each director should have full freedom to pursue his own personal style. Bergman has developed his to perfection. This does not mean that he asserts his personal standpoint in the plays he produces: he works in fact with enormous humility, changing as little as possible of the author's text. The dominant tendency as regards setting has been towards extreme simplification: the stage presents almost always a uniform colour, all unnecessary furniture and props having been removed. His *Hedda Gabler,* for instance, was played out in a red room with a sofa, a couple of chairs, a piano and a rehearsal screen as stage partition. In this way, Bergman is concerned, more than was previously possible, to emphasize the actors as the only important items on the stage. Bergman often maintains that only three things give the theatre its specific character: the actor, the subject and the audience. He succeeds also in getting his actors to demonstrate their reactions with unusual plastic clarity. Naturally, the scheme of movement must be kept utterly clear and controlled; he requires an awareness and concentration on the job that is extremely demanding, no supra-naturalistic tendencies. In his lighting, Bergman works with extreme subtlety, but he never piles new phases of lighting on top of each other: his lighting is never neurotic, but functions calmly within the often musically planned rhythm of his productions. The acting is for the most part frontal, the actors present their faces to the audience: the expression on the actors' faces in a Bergman production is often as subtle as in his films. Behind all this is a reverence for clarity, as carefully differentiated from over-clearness, and a belief in the power of words. During his period as manager of the Dramatic Theatre, Bergman had no time to stage many plays himself, but a number of his productions were memorable, including Albee's *Who's Afraid of Virginia Woolf,* which was produced in an entirely grey room. The Swedish lyric writer Harry Martinson's *Three Knives from Wei* mirrored the exposed state of mankind in the Chinese ladies-in-waiting exiled to the desert during the cruel reign of the Empress Shimoo in the

36

Hedda Gabler by Henrik Ibsen. Directed by Ingmar Bergman. Hedda Gabler — Gertrud Fridh, Jörgen Tesman — Ingvar Kjellson. Royal Dramatic Theatre, 1964.

Three Knives from Wei by Harry Martinson. Directed by Ingmar Bergman. Royal Dramatic Theatre, 1964.

7th century B. C. The last production by Bergman during his term as manager was Peter Weiss' dramatic oratorio *The Investigation,* in a stylized court room in which the entire acting space was clad in natural wood. The impression of cold hardness was further emphasized by the use of all the theatre's spotlights. The auditorium lights were left on throughout the performance, the audience was to be left no retreat. He subsequently pursued this entirely personal style in the autumn of 1966 in Molière's *School of Marriage* at the Royal Dramatic Theatre and Pirandello's *Six Characters in Search of an Author* at the National Theatre in Oslo. Bergman employs neither mysticism nor symbols, he is concerned to have the drama emerge as clearly and logically as possible: no moments of uncertainty must be permitted. One cannot, however, speak of a Brechtian *Verfremdung,* the roles are shaped with empathy — but sparsely and concentratedly. As a man of the theatre Bergman is above all a practitioner: he is concerned to work as simply and with as little extravagance as possible. Some call this classicism, Bergman himself tends to talk of the Shakespearian theatre as his ideal.

A landmark in Swedish drama

An important contribution to modern drama has been made by Bengt Ekerot, whose productions show an unusual sensitivity and care, a clear musicality and perfect respiration. Ekerot has interested himself greatly in Beckett, but his best-remembered productions have been in the chiselled naturalistic tradition, above all the world premières of O'Neill's *Long Day's Journey into Night* and *Hughie*.

The Investigation by Peter Weiss. Directed by Ingmar Bergman. Royal Dramatic Theatre, 1966.

Just the world première of Eugene O'Neill's *Long Day's Journey into Night* at the Dramatic Theatre in 1956 was one of the really important events of recent Swedish theatre. O'Neill's drama proved to be one of the masterpieces of modern literature, and Bengt Ekerot's production reached almost the level of the play. He had at his disposal the most outstanding Swedish actors of this century: James Tyrone was played by Lars Hanson, his wife by Inga Tidblad, the alcoholic son by Ulf Palme and the consumptive by Jarl Kulle.

Some Swedish Actors

Lars Hanson (1886–1965) was surely the greatest actor of the Swedish theatre, in the same inevitable way as Olof Molander was its greatest director. He worked along a single line, drawn by the Strindbergian drama. His collaboration with Olof Molander was extremely painful, but gave brilliant results. Hanson had the opportunity to play all the great roles in Strindberg's dream plays: the Stranger in *To Damascus,* the Hunter in *The Great Highway,* Hummel in *The Ghost Sonata* and the Officer in *A Dream Play*. He led the proud development of the Swedish theatre in the genre of psychological naturalism, but he always lent his characters something beyond normality. He was a master in recreating himself on the stage, in his physical dimensions, and he was surely unsurpassed in the art of make-up. In his closing years Hanson reached new heights in *Long Day's Journey into Night* and as Cornelius Melody in *A Touch of a Poet*. One of his last roles was Krapp in *Krapp's Last Tape* by Beckett.

Inga Tidblad's interpretation of Mary Tyrone was something new in this great actress's career. Her most outstanding successes have otherwise been noted in Shakespearian comedy: the clarity, grace and intelligence she has shown as

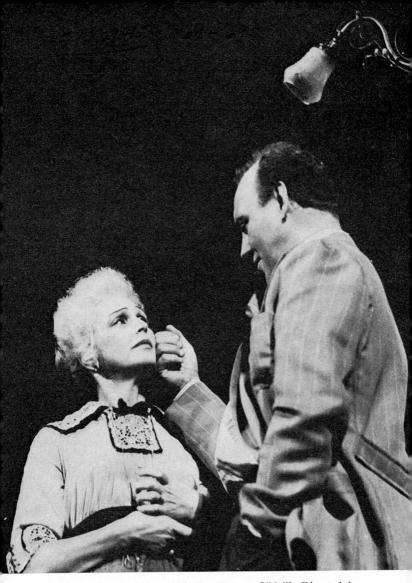

Long Day's Journey into Night by Eugene O'Neill. Directed by Bengt Ekerot. Mary Tyrone — Inga Tidblad, James Tyrone Jr. — Ulf Palme. Royal Dramatic Theatre, 1956.

Rosalinda, Beatrice and Viola in *As You Like it, Much Ado About Nothing* and *Twelfth Night* are unsurpassed.

Ulf Palme made his début in the mid-1940s, and attracted at once more attention than any other actor of his generation: his force, like Hanson's, lay in the psychological drama. He has given outstanding performances as Jean against Inga Tidblad's Miss Julie, as Erik XIV, and as Hjalmar Ekdahl in Ibsen's *Wild Duck*. His absolute peak has remained, still, the alcoholic young Tyrone.

Tora Teje took in fact no part in *Long Day's Journey into Night* but she has given brilliant performances of O'Neill roles in *Strange Interlude* and — as Christine Mannon — in *Mourning Becomes Electra*. She is the Swedish theatre's leading tragedienne, and is of the few who have succeeded in combining an unreserved passion for psychological truth with a richness and expansive force of emotion that lends her figures the enlarged measurements demanded by the classical style. Yet she has succeeded, the whole time, in persuading the audience to experience her characters as modern women.

The Swedish Theatre Today

The Swedish theatre in the 1960s is in a period of transformation: it has tired of the grand, realistic tradition that prevailed unchallenged for several decades. Discussion on the future of the theatre is unusually lively in the daily press, and an increasing number of new directors have emerged in the past few years. None of these have yet made a name for themselves, but we should mention Lars Engström in Gothenburg, who has interested himself above all in the socially committed theatre. He has staged the young Englishmen, and successfully produced also a number of new Swedish plays. His most discussed success was Bo Sköld's play of young hot-rodders *My Beloved One Is a Rose,* in which Engström enjoyed the great advantage of working with a well-knit company of young actors, who knew each other socially, who had a common language and who at once understood each others' intentions. Since he left Gothenburg, Engström has continued to work with well-knit groups of actors, most recently in the National Touring Theatre. Precisely this tendency to let a small group with a common idea work together for a prolonged period under one director in several productions has been one of the most important features of the reorientation of the Swedish theatre.

To give full reign to playfulness, to avoid fixing the moves too early, to improvise on the given text — these ideas have proved highly successful not only in Gothenburg but also in Malmö, where Ingmar Bergman's pupil

Chips with Everything by Arnold Wesker. Directed by Lennart Olsson. Malmö City Theatre, 1964.

Lennart Olsson has had a similar group to work with. Here too the inspiration has been provided by the young English drama. Wesker's *Chips with Everything,* Theatre Workshop's *Oh, What a Lovely War* and now, most recently, *Schweik in the Second World War* were unconventional productions, in which technique and freedom were carried so far that the actors exchanged roles from night to night. Malmö has one of the three state academies of drama, and instruction even at this stage now aims at similar results. The Malmö Academy has been managed since the autumn of 1967 by Lars Engström.

Stockholm too has a representative of the new, informal style — Johan Bergenstråhle at the Stockholm City Theatre, where he has taken some of the most explosive plays available and given us still more explosive productions. The violently committed American drama has been staged at the Stockholm City Theatre by Sten Lonnert, with for instance Jack Gelber's *The Connection* and Kenneth Brown's *The Brig.*

Group theatre activities have been even livelier in 1966—67. The National Touring Theatre took over Bertil Lundén's "Free Theatre", a semi-professional group that had previously been working without financial support. In Gothenburg, a team under Kent Andersson and Lennart Hjulström created its own play, and its own picture of Sweden, *The Raft,* a production reflecting a new and interesting line of development at the Gothenburg City Theatre. Sten Lonnert continued working at the Stockholm City Theatre with two new American plays by Megan Terry, *Keep Tightly Closed in a Cool Dry Place* and *Viet Rock.* But the Royal Dramatic Theatre too has been deeply engaged in group work. The "Young Dramatic Theatre", originally a summer group that staged, for instance, *Green Julia* by Paul Ableman under the direction of Niklas Brunius, has developed into a number of experimental groups that in their free

44

The Screens by Jean Genet. Directed by Per Verner-Carlsson. Stockholm City Theatre, 1964. Gerd Hagman as the Mother.

afternoons devote themselves to new forms of theatre. Notable was Staffan Roos' *Circus Madigan,* staged by the author himself.

A much debated production appeared at the Stockholm City Theatre in the spring of 1964. A young director, Per Verner-Carlsson, who had then been active with the Stockholm City Theatre throughout its brief history, but who had previously been occupied mainly with student players and radio theatre, produced for the first time the whole of Jean Genet's voluminous script for *The Screens*. It was a monumental performance, five hours long. The audience had the possibility of splitting their attendance over two evenings. The result was uneven but magnificent, and provided the starting-point for much of the now very lively debate on the theatre in the Swedish daily press. The drama of ideas and the political drama are an important aspect of modern theatre.

Lars-Erik Liedholm, who was long active at the Hälsingborg City Theatre, achieved there an extremely interesting version of Kafka's *The Trial* — with masses of roles that had to be handled by only ten actors — and a clean, clear production of Ibsen's *Brand*. He is a keen champion of Arnold Wesker's work, and the late Swedish première of the latter's first play *Chicken Soup with Barley* gave us, under his direction, a memorable theatre evening, applauded and discussed in all political camps.

In the spring of 1967, film director Bo Widerberg directed his first play for the Royal Dramatic Theatre, Albee's *A Delicate Balance;* this was an outstandingly consistent and unified production, characterized by the same subdued tone — without loss of dramatic expression — as Widerberg had previously shown in two productions for the Stockholm City Theatre, Albee's *Zoo Story* and Strindberg's *Pariah,* productions so convincing that they have become standard measures, as it were, in current discussion on the theatre.

It is not so easy to speak of the new Swedish actors: there are many young talents but the line of development is unclear. The strong influence of the new drama creates an attitude in the actor, but it is not so easy for him to express it as it is for the director. At present, a new generation of actors is growing up across a broad front. These new actors are characterized by the objectiveness with which they approach their roles and their work as a whole: for the first time, the interpretation of a role can be discussed in clear language, nothing is made more mysterious than it has to be. A new awareness has arisen; the interpretation of a role should never mystify the audience: the different sides of a figure, it is thought, should preferably be illustrated separately. This means a somewhat lower level of empathy.

Lidner by Bengt af Klintberg. Lidner — Lars-Göran Carlsson. Pistolteatern, 1966.

The purely experimental schools have few disciples in Sweden, but a very important group led by among others Pi Lind och Staffan Olzon is working at the Pistolteatern in Stockholm, where some excellent results have been achieved on the technical side. This group works above all with combinations of stage actors, films, projections and sound montage. No really great work with the exception of Bengt af Klintberg's *Lidner* has yet been created by the Pistol group, but the stimulus it provides has been of great importance for the conventional theatres.

The absolute counterpole to the Pistolteatern is the unique Drottningholm Theatre, a court theatre that was inaugurated in 1766 and where King Gustaf III about ten years later gave himself free reign with his own plays and productions. Its auditorium, scenic machinery and sets have been left entirely unchanged. Opera of the time is now played there every summer, and the theatre is a popular tourist attraction.

Swedish opera has traditions dating back to the 18th century, since Gustaf III's reform of the theatre was designed entirely to promote a national musical drama. Swedish opera today lives up to its proud traditions, and attracts also international interest, most recently at EXPO 67 in Montreal.

Ingmar Bergman's production of Stravinsky's *Rake's Progress* was one of the great operatic achievements. Otherwise, of course, Swedish opera is best known for its outstanding singers, such as Jussi Björling and Birgit Nilsson.

Swedish opera would be worth a book to itself, but there is unfortunately no space in this article for further descriptions of individual performances.

The Marionette Theatre in Stockholm, which is run by Michael Meschke, works not only with marionettes but with dolls of up to life-size and also with live actors. The theatre has presented a series of outstanding children's performances, but it caters also for adult audiences. The theatre's greatest artistic victory was its King Ubu, one of the most important productions of the 60s, which won prizes abroad. In the autumn of 1966, the group made a long tour in the United States.

Radio and television

Since the end of the 1920s, the radio has been a very important "channel of distribution" for the theatre. Our provincial theatres were long few and far between and the radio theatre became the "poor man's theatre", offering both the classics and new plays. The majority of leading Swedish writers have written radio plays. Very few have tried their hand as stage dramatists. Possibly the closeness of the radio drama to lyrical forms of expression has made

48

King Ubu by Alfred Jarry. Directed by Michael Meschke. Characters: Franciszka Themerson. Ubu — Allan Edwall. Marionette Theatre, 1964.

it particularly congenial to Swedish authors, who frequently work from lyrical starting-points. Its ease of movement, its weightlessness, and the central importance of the words, particularly in the form of metaphor and simile, have made the Swedish radio drama a highly "visual" art. But the difficulties experienced by Swedish authors in adapting their free-wheeling radio style to the strict requirements of the stage have been very pronounced. The interest in radio dramas has declined in the past eight years, since the TV Theatre has become the predominant public medium. The radio theatre has specialized to a greater extent than previously in original plays, preferably by young foreign and Swedish experimentalists, although the great classics continued to be produced. Naturally enough, the Elizabethan drama has remained very dear to the hearts of the public, being so to speak a sort of radio drama *in spe*. The TV Theatre has not found it so easy to recruit writers: the attempts made have been few and in most cases less than successful.

Johan Bergenstråhle has shown himself the really important director in Swedish TV theatre, with an outstanding ability to combine a relaxed direction of both dialogue and picture. The fears entertained by the live theatres when the TV Theatre emerged in earnest at the end of the 1950s have proved entirely unjustified. The fantastic ability of television to bring the theatre into the home seems rather to have inspired many who were previously afraid to go to the Dramatic Theatre or the municipal theatres to venture at last to a public performance, where their appetites have been whetted. The class barriers to the theatre are being broken down — although very slowly.

Training

The training of actors in Sweden is now being entirely re-organized. Dramatic training was previously given almost exclusively at the Dramatic Theatre and some of the mu-

Herr Dardanell and His Caprices by August Blanche. Directed by Johan Bergenstråhle and with Inga Gill, Olle Andersson and Gunnar Sjöberg. TV production by the Swedish Broadcasting Corporation (Sveriges Radio), 1965.

nicipal theatres: it has now been broken loose and given an independent status directly under the Ministry of Education. There are now three state academies of drama, in Stockholm, in Gothenburg and Malmö. Training lasts for three years. Other lines of theatrical training have unfortunately not yet been organized in this exemplary manner. The trainee still works as apprentice to his "master", whose job he subsequently takes over: an arrangement reminiscent of the 17th century. A state commission is now preparing forms of training for directors, decorators and make-up artists, but no one has yet interested themselves in such important categories as stage managers, lighting managers and props managers. It is extremely unfortunate that these people cannot yet look forward to any organized training.

Taking stock

In many ways, the initial position of the Swedish theatre is very good. Financially our theatres are well supported by the state, and socially stage people have reached the level of our society in general. Young actors employed at the Dramatic Theatre in 1966—67 had to begin with at least SKr 1,450 (about US $280 or £ 100) a month. Artistically speaking, the standard of the Swedish municipal theatres is high: the audiences are offered valuable theatre, both classics and current new plays. Productions maintain a heartening level. The standard of acting is even, thanks to the 3-year training undergone by most: we have no "actor proletariat" to speak of. Few actors reach the grand incomes offered to the international stars, but their work is highly varied, in that the same actors work concurrently on the stage, in radio and television and in films, the majority, however, having their main source of income from the legitimate stage. A visit to the theatre in Sweden is relatively inexpensive: thanks to subsidies, the best seats at the Dramatic

The Misanthrope by Molière. Directed by Ingmar Bergman. Alceste — Max von Sydow. Malmö City Theatre, 1957.

Theatre can be sold for SKr 16.— (just over $ 3 or £ 1), but tickets are available for as little as 3.—. This favourable position has given the municipal theatre companies an outstanding firmness, and the audience is just as faithful. To some extent as the result of this, a critical observer experiences the Swedish theatre as something rather static: our theatre people and their audiences are conservative, new ideas take a long time to penetrate. There is little on the repertory to take your breath away and our audiences, in their inertia, are not concerned to be "shaken up", even if it is not many decades since Ibsen tore into respectable Swedish theatre-goers. The traditional theatre still has the majority of advocates, and the approach to theatre-going tends to be "culinary": in the past two years, however, there has been a gradual shift of interest, towards the acceptance of newer and formally more difficult drama.

Pessimism, even so, is fairly rife among our artists, "cultural workers" and politicians. Many believe that the theatre is in its death-throes, and that the forum to which future audiences turn will be the television theatre. They believe that the subjects handled by the theatre can be presented in a manner more suitable to modern audiences in a television production, both as *rapportage* and fiction. This belief says something important: the theatre can never be a living phenomenon if it does not adopt a position to its time and to its society. It can easily become a historical monument. Every production must imply the adoption of a position. The mediation of news today, in all its forms, has offered the theatre inspiration and rejuvenation also formally. Television, for instance, has trained the public to see programmes in which documentary and fictitious material are mixed, a pattern subsequently pursued in the modern drama. An example is Peter Weiss' *Marat-Sade*. Obviously, the television can in time teach its audience also to react critically, and an increased awareness seems already to be emerging:

but for it to be further developed, it is necessary that the TV Theatre be widened, that it abandon its ambitions to be a stage theatre, ambitions which bar the way to a more interesting repertory.

If the government could only realize now that the provincial theatres must be expanded, then our most important problem would have been solved. It is not enough to have eight municipal theatres — we must have them in all our towns. The reorganization of the National Touring Theatre should be an outstanding help in this respect. With a greater use of group theatre, teams can be assigned to base towns in the provinces and subsequently develop into circuit or municipal theatres. Such a system is already lined up for Västerås and Örebro. A rapid solution is necessary, in view of the fact that our three dramatic academies will be spitting out more and more actors every year. Finland has solved the problem in a rational manner: each town there has its theatre, the actors are few in number, as are the company's other staff. To have its own theatre means a great deal to a town, both socially and culturally. The continuous contact with the artists provides a far greater stimulus than a company of strangers arriving in the town for two or three days. The municipal theatres in the university towns should be able to establish cooperation with the local student theatre. This could surely give rise to an exciting experimental drama in the student theatre. In general, it should be possible in this way to utilize more efficiently the emerging resources that tend otherwise to be wasted. Each theatre would serve not only its own town, but as wide a surrounding area as possible. It is important, too, that the combination "bus or train trip/theatre visit" be studied. It must be easy for the audience to get to the theatre: this type of problem has to be solved above all in Norrland, where the distances involved mean often whole-day trips. An expansion of the activities of municipal theatres in the rural districts will naturally reduce the importance of the National Touring Theatre.

The Swedish educational system is at present being thoroughly reorganized. If we are to achieve an increased cultural awareness, then aesthetic education must be given its fair share of the curriculum. In the case of the theatre, it is possible to envisage a basic foundation on which to develop. We should first accustom small children to visiting the theatre: in the larger towns this presupposes an independent, generously financed and properly equipped children's theatre with good actors. To follow this up, it should be possible for all young people, including working young people under 21, to see regular theatre performances at a greatly reduced price. This system has already been tried in Stockholm, with great success.

In a short survey like this, I have had to content myself with a fairly summary account of the Swedish theatre today. What I have wanted to stress above all is the high standard attained by our theatre throughout the country, and at the same time the great changes that are taking place — changes that are obviously necessary, but the results of which it is difficult to foresee.

GÖRAN O ERIKSSON

The General Gets its Caviar

For the first time in many years, we have begun in the mid-1960s to discuss the problem of the theatre as part of our social policy at large; some consider, in fact, that the theatre is doomed by virtue of its social circumstances, while others consider that it has a chance to play a more important role in society by calling precisely these circumstances into question. The problem of how this is to be achieved has been discussed above all by the new generation of critics that has emerged in this decade. This discussion, I think, throws more light on the altered status of the theatre in Sweden today than do the policies of individual theatres, and I should like therefore briefly to sketch in the background.

Let us, to begin with, take as our example a theatre manager who has helped bring about the change, by exploiting a given economic situation to the utmost. Namely Ingmar Bergman.

Bergman was manager at the Royal Dramatic Theatre from 1963 to 1966, and he left his mark on it. He has since said that he now regards those years as a failure. This they were not. He did not, it is true, complete refashion his theatre, but he succeeded in setting it free — and the liberation of the Dramatic Theatre was representative of development in the Swedish theatre as a whole. This liberation was of two kinds, economic and aesthetic. Its impetus was a rapid and radical expansion of state support to the arts.

A radical increase in state grants to the arts had been initiated in the early 1960s, and by 1965 it was largely completed. The reform was not restricted to the theatre; it provided at least a temporary solution to the lack of security of individual actors — and writers, composers and artists — by the creation of quite a large number of "artists' awards", which functioned as financial guarantees in the event of improductivity or difficulties in selling their work; it provided for greater support to museums, libraries, concert societies, and cultural activities in general. Sweden had been built up materially, it was time to start on the spirit.

So far as the theatre was concerned, this meant a strong and immediately perceptible increase in resources. During Bergman's brief period as manager, state grants to the Dramatic Theatre went up by about SKr 6 million, to almost 9 million. At the same time, state support to the Swedish theatre reached in the fiscal year 1965—66 almost SKr 55 million; this sum includes 3 million to the state theatre schools, but not the above-mentioned guarantees to individual artists.

This was a violent and effective expansion. It did not, however, have any pronounced socio-political aim. It was a direct consequence of social development as a whole. The arts were regarded as a market, with producers, distributors and consumers, the latter having previously been drawn from the privileged classes. It was now desired to offer the same opportunities for consumption to everyone, precisely as in other sectors. At the same time, a new problem had arisen. The demand for entertainment, both light and serious, had grown during the 1950s in step with the general rise in standard-of-living, and had attracted more persons than previously to the theatrical occupations; there was a sudden risk of saturation, with a new proletariat of creative artists as the result. This risk too had to be met by a stepping-up of economic resources.

One of Ingmar Bergman's most striking productions at the Dramatic Theatre was Albee's *Who's Afraid of Virginia Wolf?* Here Bibi Andersson and Karin Kavli.

There was no discussion of the nature of the product. Nor of its tendency. In setting priorities, the state followed instead, as far as possible, the desires of the artists themselves, as expressed by their professional organizations. The government thought it was implementing a cultural policy; in fact it was applying already existing socio-political principles to occupational categories that it had previously been impossible to incorporate in the development of the welfare state. Nothing more.

Increased job opportunities, in other words, higher wages, greater social security for the theatre's employees — but also bigger companies, a heavier administration, and a greater latent unemployment. More actors were employed on annual contracts only to be kept in reserve, without working more than perhaps two or three months a year. Their economic security was so far ensured, but not their artistic development. They had been given more time for further training; but such further training was neglected, since its aims were not specified.

It is this situation that is exemplified by Ingmar Bergman's work as manager at the Dramatic Theatre, and which makes it symptomatic. His work had a radiant brilliance, an atmosphere of magnificence, ease, and generosity to the point of waste, as long as it was his own theatre he was concerned with. He saw his task as one gigantic production, with the serried ranks of Swedish actors from which to cast. He wanted, he said, to make his theatre "the best there is", the most magnificent in Sweden or in the world. He made it more clearly a "repertory theatre" than before, and at the same time he expanded the number of newly purchased plays. He engaged actors without worrying unduly about what happened at the theatres to which they had previously been attached, and he was able in this way radically to renew his own company. Working from this citadel of talent, he started touring in the provinces, an activity that he intended to build up on a national scale. More than any of his predecessors, he turned directly to the young audiences, and made it possible for them to visit the theatre at reasonable prices. Under his management, the Dramatic Theatre became an institution where nothing should be lacking; its purpose being to give the best possible to as many as possible as quickly as possible.

At that time, the same mood of "no limits" was reflected in almost everything attempted in Sweden; this mood was not subdued before the tighter economic situation of 1966.

Aesthetically, this expansion was undoubtedly a sort of liberation. The Dramatic Theatre — which after the war entirely dominated the style of Swedish theatre — had long

Jarl Kulle, Lars Hanson and Ulf Palme in Bengt Ekerot's production of O'Neill's *Long Day's Journey into Night,* the most distinguished of the great O'Neill productions that were the culmination of the psychological, realistic style of acting at the Royal Dramatic Theatre.

played in an Ibsenist tradition, a virtuoso presentation of the tensions between action and motive, a style in which one could still feel the Ibsenist theatre's conflict between hidden feeling and overt attitudes to be sufficient motivation for a production, a satisfying pattern to demonstrate on the stage. Psychoanalysis, in other words, was still taken seriously as a theory of art. This style of theatre culminated in a succession of brilliant productions of O'Neill's last plays, which the author himself had wanted to have their première on the Stockholm stage. The last, *Build More Stately Mansions,* opened as recently as in the autumn of 1962.

Bergman broke with all this — not by offering any alternative, but by radically broadening the theatre's artistic range. He himself, it is true, staged Ibsen, but with such a personal reading that his production resembled more a polemic against the earlier style than a development of it. He had Alf Sjöberg stage Brecht, whom the theatre had previously neglected, but without for an instant making the Dramatic Theatre a Brechtian stage: Sjöberg's Brecht interpretations likewise showed their strength more in a subjective power of creation than in theoretical consistency. All this meant simply a widening of the framework. This was indeed enough, since it was more than it seemed: it meant that an aesthetic obstacle to the social expansion of the theatre had been removed. Acting need no longer be regarded as an artistic device for the repetition of psychoanalytic interpretations of characters in a closed and unchangeable environment.

At the same time, it is clear that this break could not lead directly to a more socially critical theatre than previously. It simply altered the background conditions for social criticism from the stage, since it brought up questions of stage realism that had previously been discussed only sporadically in Sweden. This entire swing corresponded to an international development in the literature and literary theory of the 1950s, and it had begun to be noticeable in the theatre even before its implementation at the Dramatic Theatre, in individual productions out in the provinces, and at Stockholm's other theatres. I personally experienced the change most clearly in a TV production of Lorca's *Doña Rosita, the Spinster,* broadcast in 1960 with Ulla Sjöblom in the title role. Eight years previously, one of the Dramatic Theatre's leading actresses, Inga Tidblad, had played the same role. The "living lie" was then still in fashion; there was thus portrayed a Rosita who was false, or at least ambiguous, a Rosita whose faithfulness was a schizophrenic flight into unreality. This indeed was how Lorca regarded her: as a victim. But in Ulla Sjöblom the role assumed another meaning. She had understood that Rosita lives in an absence, not in a lie. She could therefore give the role a homogeneity and factualness that it had previously lacked: she made her live as an individual, not as a problem. Only a few years previously, such a portrayal would have seemed one-sided, insipid, perhaps intellectually bare. In the short time between these two productions it had become true.

It is changes of this type that provided a starting-point for the new theatrical criticism of the 1960s. The number of

A scene from Alf Sjöberg's production of Gombrowicz' *The Marriage* (1966), with Birgitta Valberg and Ernst-Hugo Järegård as the parents and Jan-Olof Strandberg as Henrik.

these critics is not large. They are all young. They all work in Stockholm, on a couple of the big daily papers and in the group around the magazine "Dialog", which was first published in 1965. They are all university graduates. The majority of them are literary critics, and some of them are consciously trying to apply the methods of modern textual criticism to acting and direction. They are consequently regarded with suspicion both by their older colleagues and by the actors and directors, who consider that the theatre can be judged only from their own premises. On one point these critics differ markedly from their predecessors: they do not hesitate to seek up contacts with the theatre, and their activity expresses rather a feeling of solidarity with the artists of the theatre, than any position of opposition. The main task these critics set themselves is not the assessment of individual productions. Their main theme is the relationship of the theatre to its public, and one of the reasons for their emergence in the past five years is that the conflict between the theatre's needs and those of society has during this time become acute.

The economic expansion of the 1960s has not, by itself, been able to alter the relationship between theatre and public. It is still a prestige-conferring action to go to the theatre in Sweden: the result of the economic reform was at most that more people had a chance of identifying themselves with the privileged groups, just as more people could afford to run a car or have a house of their own. This is a change, but it has nothing to do with the nature of theatrical experience, and the question is whether the change is even desirable. As long as the prestige of the theatrical experience overshadows its content, it is difficult to speak of a living, democratic theatrical culture.

How can we achieve anything beyond this?

The country is still being urbanized; at the same time, the big towns are being decentralized. We are getting a

Per Hjern and John Ekman in Knut Ström's production of *The Merchant of Venice* in 1936, the most famous of the great productions at Gothenburg City Theatre in the 1930s.

heterogeneous urban public, spread out over the wide surfaces covered by the new agglomerations of building. The theatres in the centre have very little to do with this peripheral population — other than as a season-ticket audience — and they therefore have difficulty in serving as an instrument for it.

So, the theatre must be decentralized, autonomous companies must be set up immediately adjacent to the environment — place of work or residential area — where it is to function, in order that actors may be able to fulfil the task that is most important *in the present situation,* namely to get the people of the new towns to participate in their own history.

This is why the new critics are sceptical of the "folk thea-tre" thinking that still characterizes the theatre policy of the social democrats in Sweden. They find it passive, and thus conservative. This does not mean they want political pro-ductions, or a theatre of pure agitation. On the contrary, they believe that agitation can have a disastrous effect on acting — and that it is on the actors, not on the directors, that a decentralized theatre must be based.

A practical expression of this desire to decentralize was the proposal for a new city theatre in Stockholm jointly presented by a group of critics and dramatic artists in the spring of 1967.

The question of a new city theatre in Stockholm had al-ready been under discussion for many years. The city theatre, since its creation, has played in provisory premises in the centre of town, premises unsatisfactory both for the actors and for audiences; thus far everyone has been in agreement.

The local authority has seen the solution in a new, large theatre building in the centre of the town, with facilities of sufficient flexibility to permit practically all conceivable sorts of theatre activity. Drawings for such a theatre have been presented by one of the country's leading theatre architects, Professor Sven Markelius. His proposal is in many ways entirely admirable, but it does not solve what the critics consider to be the main problem: to bring the theatre and its audiences closer together.

We have here in fact two opposing policies. The one is reflected to some extent both in the commission given by the city to Professor Markelius and in his execution of it. It is mainly pedagogical; it identifies the need of the public with a need for combined entertainment and instruction: a need of ready productions perfectly staged in an attractive framework. The great merit of Markelius' proposal is in-deed that it offers a possibility of meeting practically all

John Osborne's *Look Back in Anger* had its Swedish première at the Gothenburg City Theatre in 1957, produced by Åke Falck and with Gun Arvidsson as Alison, Jan-Olof Strandberg as Cliff, and Keve Hjelm as Jimmy Porter.

conceivable variations of this need. It is difficult to see in his proposal any attempt to change either the structure of the audience, or the relationship of the present audience to the theatre.

The other approach is that reflected in the counterproposals of the group of critics and theatre people. For them, the essential point is that new and natural contacts should be established between theatrical production and the public that today has no access to the theatrical experience — primarily for social reasons, as clear from a sociological study of the leisure pursuits of Stockholmers made by Docent Harald Swedner. The group further considers that the current rejuvenation of the theatre lies more in the action than in the design of stage facilities, and that it is in the action that these new contacts with audiences can arise. They are following here the tendencies in modern dramatic training that have begun to be realized also at the Swedish theatre schools (so far mainly at the state Dramatic Academy in Malmö).

Their argument, in other words, is as follows. The City Theatre's need for a large, technically satisfactory stage must be met as soon as possible. It is equally important, however, that the town have stages that make it possible to perform as far as possible in the immediate vicinity of the residential and working environments. Finally, the town needs a permanent stage for children's theatre. To realize this plan, it is proposed that a number of existing stages — private and public — in the inner and peripheral areas of the town be managed as a chain under a central administrative management, but with separate artistic managements, separate annual grants within the framework of the municipal theatre organization, and — to some extent — separate companies. In this chain, the new building for the City Theatre should be incorporated as one link among others, even if it has a considerably larger seating and acting capacity. To sum up, a new building with two stages in the city centre, as part of a chain of theatres in the inner and outer areas, for which there will be exploited certain existing facilities, while others will be designed in the areas now lacking a stage. Each of these theatres — including the new

Peter Weiss' *Marat-Sade* was played 1966—67 in three widely different productions in Stockholm, Malmö and Gothenburg. Here a scene from Ralf Långbacka's Brechtian production at the Gothenburg City Theatre, with Margaretha Löwler as Corday and Roland Hedlund as Marat.

city stages — should have their own artistic manager, and their own annual budget. The entire municipal theatre organization has a joint company of actors, but it is conceivable either that each of the theatres in the chain should be able to recruit a basic permanent company for a certain period, plus such supplementary actors as it may need in different situations — or else that the entire company be split up over the different theatres, which would still presuppose a greater degree of mobility than now, with openings for the exchange and supplementation of actors between theatres.

The core of this proposal is obviously that the need of the city theatre in Stockholm should be understood not as the need for a new building, but as the need for a coordinated administration of the town's theatrical life — an administration that can continuously follow the growth of the town out into the surrounding countryside. The artistic resources to realize such a development already exist. The economic resources are also available. But what of our theoretical resources?

Less than ever is it possible today to formulate a collective theory for the Swedish theatre. The theatre seems to have shaken off all the theories that for so many years — with or without the intentions of its directors — determined the view of man presented in its productions, and in the work of individual actors. Today, it is very much an extrovert theatre.

What gives the Swedish theatre its vitality, its limitations, and — paradoxically enough — its peculiar character, is above all its consistent eclecticism. It is open to all impulses, and it takes them all as true. It catches up dramatic innovations the world over, and commits itself to them with a lack of hesitation that bears witness to a considerable artistic and emotional capacity.

At the same time, this theatre has for decades been

Staffan Aspelin's production of Chekhov's *Three Sisters* in 1966, a lyrical, realistic interpretation at the Gothenburg City Theatre, with Margita Ahlin, Lisa Bergström and Kerstin Tidelius.

Sten Lonnert's productions of off-Broadway drama — Jack Gelber's *The Connection*, Megan Terry's *Keep Tightly Closed in a Cool Dry Place* and *Viet Rock* — have largely set the tone at the Stockholm City Theatre during the 1960s. Here Carl-Olof Alm in *The Connection*.

strangely isolated in the Swedish intellectual debate. It has turned outwards more to the international world of the theatre, than to the politics and aesthetics of other countries; and to a corresponding degree, Swedish writers and critics have until the past two or three years neglected the theatre, looked down their noses at it, or ignored it. Consequently we have had a shortage of Swedish playwrights of any calibre, since they have had no natural environment to work in. Of the writers leaving their mark on Swedish post-war literature, only Lars Forssell, really, has exploited dramatic means of expression, and this successfully.

The situation is now changing. In the latter 1950s young

writers discovered the film and intellectualized it — first in France, then in a number of other countries, everywhere that the sophisticated public was sufficiently large to carry a production of this kind. Today we are seeing a new wave in the theatre. This involves, as in the cinema, an increased interest in formal problems, parallel with a realism that rejects the anecdotal as a false interpretation and sees the actor as the primary aspect of the production. At the Stockholm City Theatre, this tendency has been reflected in a succession of excellent productions of new American off-Broadway drama, directed by Sten Lonnert: including Megan Terry's *Keep Tightly Closed in a Cool Dry Place* and *Viet Rock,* and earlier Jack Gelber's *The Connection.*

It is as if the theatre had suddenly been thrown up to the young writers, as if it had begun to speak their language. They have responded by committing themselves to the thea-

Megan Terry's *Viet Rock,* directed by Sten Lonnert. Here Yvonne Lombard and Hans Bendrik. Stockholm City Theatre, 1967.

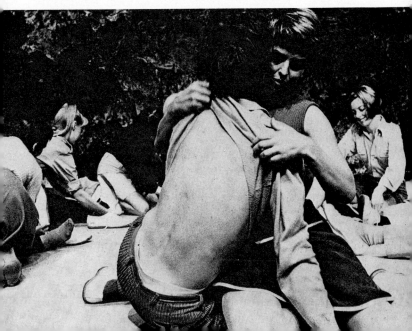

tre. At once, we have young playwrights working in intimate cooperation with directors and actors, when they are not their own directors: Sven Delblanc, Staffan Roos, Sandro Key-Åberg, Bengt Bratt and others. In Stockholm, the little Pistolteatern — privately owned, but enjoying considerable financial support from the City Council — has been the pioneer for this new interplay between the stage and its writers. It has interested itself to a high degree in topical material: when the Ben Barka affair was at its height, it was presented there in a very free production, and this spring the theatre's manager, Pi Lind, presented a revue-type play in which the Greek coup d'état had been given a Swedish setting, to make it comprehensible for a Swedish audience without any great experience of violent change.

There is some evidence, however, that the most remarkable development in the Swedish theatre during the next ten years will take place at the municipal theatres in the provinces. We now have eight such theatres, run on central and local government support. Two of them serve at the same time a neighbouring town. The most recent, that in Luleå, was inaugurated this autumn. Together with the National Touring Theatre, it is these stages that have the best chance of establishing contact with the great bulk of the population who today never visit a theatre — and which therefore have the best chance of giving this rich and perplexed theatre a direction and content. Their actors are recruited predominantly from the dramatic academies in Stockholm, Gothenburg and Malmö. Dramatic training — above all at the Malmö school, run during its early years by Georg Fant, now manager of the Luleå Regional Theatre, and Andris Blekte — has developed in many ways more rapidly than the theatre itself, partly because the layman influence is less at the schools than on the municipal stages. We are right up in a process of change, and we have the resources to carry it through; whether the change will be successful, and give results, will depend largely on the ability of the critics and the politicians to formulate the aims of the new theatre.

ROLF REMBE

The State, the Theatres and the Actors

Sweden's private theatres find themselves in much the same situation as the private theatres in other modern societies. In other words, they are having financial difficulties. Box-office receipts are insufficient to cover the increased overheads for premises, publicity, actors and technicians. The few private theatres still in existence are almost all in Stockholm, although some of them pay occasional visits to Gothenburg and Malmö. Almost without exception, their productions belong to the realm of "light entertainment".

Those theatres which are concerned to offer a more substantial menu inevitably require some form of public subsidy in order to exist. Our earliest traditions in this respect are associated with the two royal theatres, Kungliga teatern (the Opera) and Kungliga dramatiska teatern (the Royal Dramatic Theatre), which date from the 18th century. The state is directly responsible for the finances of these theatres. The Swedish Parliament sets the frames of their budgets, the Government appoints their governing boards and managers.

At the same time, however, these theatres are independent share companies, and the theatre management has an entirely free hand in the choice of productions and "artistic" policy in general. If friction ever occurs it is of a financial nature. Ingmar Bergman, during his recent period as manager, widely and cold-bloodedly overran his budget on a couple of occasions. The Government gnashed its

Carl Erik Boström, Margareta Olsson and Sven Andrén in Claes von Rettig's production of Dario Fo's farce *Better a Thief in the House,* which together with García Lorca's *Doña Rosita, the Spinster,* opened its première in Nyköping 1967. National Touring Theatre/Swedish Theatre.

teeth — but paid the deficit as a fair price for the artistic expansion noted under Bergman's management.

The state grant received by the Opera amounts for the current fiscal year (1967/68) to SKr 17.8 million, while the Dramatic Theatre gets 9.1 million. This means that the Opera covers about 20 per cent of its overheads by box-office receipts etc., the remaining 80 per cent being covered by the state. In the case of the Dramatic Theatre, about 30 per cent of costs are met by the theatre itself and 70 per cent by the state.

Tickets are thus strongly subsidized and much cheaper

than in the private theatres. The Dramatic Theatre in particular has in recent years reduced its prices to young people, to increase the theatre-going public. All persons under 21 — not only school children and students — can now buy tickets to all seats at a price of SKr 5, without having to wait for "empty seats".

The Opera and the Dramatic Theatre are "national" theatres, but since they function in Stockholm they play mainly to audiences from the capital. Naturally enough, the rest of the country also demands that the state should provide for its theatrical needs, and such support is given in two ways: to the Riksteatern (the National Touring Theatre) and to the different municipal and city theatres.

The National Touring Theatre was created in answer to the crisis that struck private touring stock companies in the late 1920s and early 1930s. The National Touring Theatre and a couple of other state-supported touring companies quickly developed into a theatre of unique scope and character, playing at over 400 places from the north to the south of Sweden, winter and summer alike. Audiences have varied, as has the quality of stages available, but in most places the touring theatre has succeeded in building up a very lasting interest in the theatre.

Developments in the past ten years, with a migration to the built-up areas, increased motoring and the spread of television throughout the country, have put a considerable strain on the touring companies. Activities have been concentrated to the larger areas, and consolidated by the incorporation of the other state-supported touring companies into the National Touring Theatre. The state grant to that company this year amounts to SKr 13.6 million. On top of this, there are the grants made by local authorities to the local societies which purchase performances.

The municipal (or city) theatres are at present seven in number *(Malmö, Hälsingborg, Gothenburg, Borås, Norr-*

Rut Cronström and Gösta Bråhner in Lars Engström's production of Pinter's *Birthday Party,* première in Skövde, 1966. National Touring Theatre/Swedish Theatre.

köping-Linköping, Stockholm and Uppsala). State support to these theatres takes the form of a guaranteed grant of 55 per cent of the costs of pay, pensions etc. The governing bodies of these theatres are appointed by the local authorities, which meet the deficits incurred — the state grant towards pay is of course insufficient. Another two theatres in Gothenburg receive a state grant of similar type, the Gothenburg Lyric Theatre and the little Folk Theatre. The total state grant to the municipal theatres this year amounts to SKr 14.7 million.

The manager of a municipal theatre has a very free hand in deciding policy. Nor does the state make any conditions whatsoever for its support to these theatres.

In the autumn of 1967 another state-supported theatre was started in the northern town of *Luleå*. Its players will be taking over also some of the local touring performances now provided by the National Touring Theatre. The activities of the Luleå Theatre will be followed with great interest by the theatre world, since the future of the touring theatre is at present a subject of lively argument. A growing opinion maintains that touring performances should be taken to a larger extent from the permanent theatres. It is considered that both actors and producers do themselves better justice if they are permitted to work in a permanent collective, with a permanent stage as their home base. The present arrangement, by which touring companies are composed on an *ad hoc* basis is considered by many to be unsatisfactory.

About half of Sweden's c. 1,100 actors and entertainers are freelance. The other half are employed at the Opera, the Royal Dramatic Theatre and the municipal theatres, in practice with 12-month contracts. The actors, producers, stage designers and other theatre staff are organized in the Swedish Actors' Equity Association. The theatres have their employers' organization in the Swedish Theatre As-

Eva Sköld, in her production of *Romeo and Juliet* (1967), utilized the great apron stage of the Malmö City Theatre, fenced in by a two-foot high railing. Juliet — Brita-Lena Sjöberg. Right, Gunnar Ekström.

Arnold Wesker's *The Kitchen* — première in Linköping 1967 — was actor Ernst Günther's breakthrough as a director, and an enormous success for stage designer Akke Nordwall. Norrköping-Linköping Municipal Theatre.

sociation. By intensive bargaining, the actors have achieved over the past ten years a major improvement in their previously often wretched terms of employment. Parallel with this development, and partly as the result of it, the central and local government grants to theatres have undergone a considerable increase: in the past ten years, they have been roughly tripled.

The state measure that may prove in the long run to have the greatest importance for the Swedish theatre, is the improved system of dramatic training. Such training was previously incorporated in certain theatres, and its financial resources were very modest. For the training of actors there were set up in 1963 three independent 3-year schools in Stockholm, Gothenburg and Malmö. From these there will graduate every year some 40 actors. The state grant, which five years ago totalled SKr 70,000, amounts for the current fiscal year to SKr 3.2 million.

Above all in Stockholm, an important role is played by the theatre-goers' organization Skådebanan, which has greatly helped to increase the size of audiences. Skådebanan has agents at a large number of places of work and in the trade unions etc., and it can offer its members tickets to the Opera, the Dramatic Theatre, the city theatre and the private theatres at reduced prices.

The private theatres (excluding the revue theatres) are supported by the City of Stockholm, which buys annually 10 per cent of these theatres' tickets at a fixed price of

Peter Weiss' *The Lusitanian Bogeyman* had its world première in 1967 at a private theatre in Stockholm, the Scala Theatre. Directed by Etienne Glaser. Here Lena Brundin and Allan Edwall.

SKr 12 and sells them for SKr 4 to students' and old-age pensioners' societies, national servicemen and the chronically ill. The theatres concerned obtain in this way an annual grant of about SKr 650,000.

Parallel with the outward expansion of our theatres' activities (larger audiences, larger companies and more performances), a certain transformation seems to be occurring in their internal structure: the authoritarian systems of earlier decades and centuries are being discarded, and a greater measure of collective artistic decision introduced. Ingmar Bergman started his term as manager of the Dramatic Theatre by creating a council of representatives chosen by the actors themselves. This council discusses with the theatre manager all major artistic questions, including choice of productions, casting, the employment of new actors and the renewal of contracts. A similar development seems to be taking place at other theatres. The young generation believes the future of the theatre to lie in artistic cooperation within the collective of a company.

BIBLIOGRAPHY OF SWEDISH DRAMA
IN TRANSLATION

In making this bibliography the Swedish Institute has obtained information on printed material from the Royal Swedish Library. Information on material translated but not printed has been provided by the Swedish Centre of the International Theatre Institute, the Drama Department of the Swedish Broadcasting Corporation (Sveriges Radio), and Swedish publishers of dramatic works.

The bibliography is in no way selective, and contains all the translations made since 1950, which have come to our notice (Danish and Norwegian not included). We are aware that there must be many omissions, and would therefore be grateful for corrections and supplementary information, in order that subsequent editions may be more complete.

PRINTED

ENGLISH

Collections:

The Genius of the Scandinavian Theatre. Contains: Strindberg, August, To Damascus. Part 1. (Till Damaskus); Crimes and Crimes (Brott och Brott); Lagerkvist, Pär, The Difficult Hour (Den svåra stunden). 637 p. New York 1967.

Masterpieces of the Modern Scandinavian Theatre. Contains: Strindberg, August, Miss Julie (Fröken Julie); The Ghost Sonata (Spöksonaten); Lagerkvist, Pär, The Difficult Hour (Den svåra stunden). 479 p. New York 1967.

Modern Scandinavian Plays. August Strindberg, Kaj Munk, Tryggvi Sveinbjörnsson, Tryggve Kielland. 366 p. New York 1954.

Scandinavian Plays of the Twentieth Century. Ser. 3. Hjalmar Bergman, The Swedenhielms. A Comedy in Four Acts. P. 21—101; Pär Lagerkvist, Let Man Live. P. 103—121. Stig Dagerman, The Condemned. A Drama in Four Acts. P. 123—195. Transl. from the Swedish by Henry Alexander and Llewellyn Jones. 195 p. Princeton 1951.

Separate Plays:

Aspenström, Werner, The Apes Shall Inherit the Earth. Transl. by Leif Sjöberg and Randolph Goodman. P. 92—97. In: The Tulane Drama Review 1961.

Aspenström, Werner, The Poet and the Emperor. A Radio Comedy (Sw. orig.: Poeten och kejsaren 1956.) (Transl. by P. Britten Austin) Stockholm 1957.

Bergman, Hjalmar, The Swedenhielms. (Sw. orig.: Swedenhielms.: 1925). Transl. (by H. Alexander and L. Jones) P. 21—101. In: Scandinavian Plays of the Twentieth Century. Ser. 3. New York 1951.

Bergman, Ingmar, Four Screenplays of Ingmar Bergman. Transl. by Lars Malmström and David Kushner. 2. impr. 329 p. Ill. New York 1960. (Contents: Smiles of a Summer Night. The Seventh Seal. Wild Strawberries. The Magician.)

Dagerman, Stig, The Condemned. A Drama in Four Acts. (Sw. orig.: Den dödsdömde. 1947) Transl. by H. Alexander and L. Jones. P. 123—195. In: Scandinavian Plays of the Twentieth Century. Ser. 3. New York 1951.

Forsell, Lars, (Sw. orig.: Söndagspromenaden.) Oslo. Will appear.

Fridell, Folke, (Sw. orig.: Den andres bröd.) Oslo. Will appear.

Görling, Lars, (Sw. orig.: Trängningen.) Oslo. Will appear.

Hartman, Olov, Mary's Quest. A Liturgical Drama. Transl., with an introduction, by Eric J. Sharpe. (Sw. orig.: Marias oro.) 32 p. London 1963.

Höijer, Björn-Erik, (Sw. orig.: Isak Juntti hade många söner.) Oslo. Will appear.

Johansson, Arthur, The Beautiful Face of the Devil. (Sw. orig.: Bländverk.) Transl. by Kersti French. London 1963.

Johansson, Arthur, In Conference. (Sw. orig.: Sammanträde pågår.) Transl. by Kersti French. London 1963.

Johansson, Arthur, No More Stalls. (Sw. orig.: Ingen parkett.) Transl. by Kersti French. London 1963.

Johansson, Arthur, The Tin Soldier. (Sw. orig.: Tennsoldaten.) Transl. by Kersti French. London 1963.

Lagerkvist, Pär, The Difficult Hour: three one-act plays. (Den svåra stunden. Tre enaktare. Teater 1918). (In: The Tulane Drama Review, New Orleans, 6 (1961), No 2, P. 3—58.)

Lagerkvist, Pär, Let Man Live. (A Play) (Sw. orig.: Låt människan leva. 1949) Transl. by H. Alexander and L. Jones. P. 103—121. In: Scandinavian Plays of the Twentieth Century. Ser. 3. New York 1951.

Lagerkvist, Pär, Let Man Live (Låt människan leva. 1949) (In: Martin Halverson (ed.), Religious Drama 3. New York 1959; London 1960. P. 99—120.)

Lagerkvist, Pär, Midsummer Dream in the Workhouse. A Play. (Sw. orig.: Midsommardröm i fattighuset. 1941) Transl. by A. Blair. 53 p. London 1953.

Lagerkvist, Pär, Modern Theatre: Points of View and Attack. The Difficult Hour... (Sw. orig.: Den svåra stunden.) — Lamm, Martin, Strindberg and the Theatre. Transl. and with an essay, Pär Lagerkvist and the Swedish Theatre, by Thomas R. Buckman. 97 p. New Orleans 1961. (Repr. from: The Tulane Drama Review 1961.)

Lagerkvist, Pär, Modern Theatre. Seven Plays and an Essay. Transl., with an introd., by Thomas R. Buckman. The Difficult Hour I, II, III, The Secret of Heaven, The King, The Hangman, The Philosopher's Stone. (Sw. orig.: Den svåra stunden, Himlens hemlighet, Konungen, Bödeln, Den vises sten.) 305 p. Ill. Lincoln 1966.

Lindström, Rune, A Play Which Tells of a Road that Leads to Heaven. "Six Dalecarlian Wall-Paintings". (Sw. orig.: Ett spel om en väg som till himla bär. 1941) Transl. by E. H. Schubert. 100 p. Stockholm 1955.

Moberg, Vilhelm, Fulfilment. A Play in Five Acts. (Sw. orig.: Mans kvinna. 1943) Transl. by M. Herin. 74 p. London 1953.

Roos, Staffan, If the War Comes or an Exemplifying Theatrical Prospect. In: Young Cinema and Theatre, 4. 1966.

Strindberg, August
Collections:

The Chamber Plays. Storm Weather. — The Burned House. — The Ghost Sonata. — The Pelican. Transl. from the Swedish by Evert Sprinchorn, Seabury Quinn Jr., and Kenneth Petersen. (Sw. orig.: Oväder, Brända tomten, Spöksonaten, Pelikanen.) 228 p. New York 1962.

Eight Expressionist Plays. Transl. and with pref. to the Pilgrimage Plays by Arvid Paulson. Introd. and with a pref. to the Ghost Sonata by John Gassner. (Sw. orig.: Lycko-Pers resa, Himmelrikets nycklar, Till Damaskus I, II, III, Ett drömspel, Stora landsvägen, Spöksonaten.) 499 p. Toronto 1965.

Five Plays. In new transl. by Elizabeth Sprigge. (Creditors, Crime and Crime, The Dance of Death, Swanwhite, The Great Highway.) (Sw. orig.: Fordringsägare, Brott och brott, Dödsdansen, Svanevit, Stora landsvägen.) 351 p. New York 1960.

The Last of the Knights. The Regent. Earl Birger of Bjälbo. (Sw. orig.: Siste riddaren 1908. Riksföreståndaren 1909. Bjälbojarlen 1909) Transl. and introductions by W. Johnson. 257 p. Ill. Seattle 1956.

Miss Julie & Other Plays. Miss Julie, Creditors, The Ghost Sonata, The Stronger. Adapted into English by Max Faber. With an introduction by John Allen. (Sw. orig.: Fröken Julie, Fordringsägare, Spöksonaten, Den starkare.) 145 p. London 1960.

Plays. Transl. by E. Sprigge. (Contains: The Father; Miss Julie; Creditors; The Stronger; The Bond; Crime and Crime; Easter; The Dance of Death; Swanwhite; A Dream Play; The Ghost Sonata; The Great Highway). (Sw. orig.: Fadren 1887; Fröken Julie 1888; Fordringsägare 1888; Den starkare 1889; Bandet 1892; Brott och brott 1899; Påsk 1901; Dödsdansen 1901; Svanevit 1901; Ett drömspel 1901; Spöksonaten 1907; Stora landsvägen 1909). 689 p. Chicago 1962. (With the title:) Twelve Plays. 689 p. London 1963.

The Plays. Introduced and transl. from the Swedish by Michael Meyer. London: Mercury Books. Vol 1. (The Father. — Miss Julie. — Creditors. — The Stronger. — Playing with Fire. — Erik the Fourteenth. — Storm. — The Ghost Sonata. Sw. orig.: Fadren. — Fröken Julie. — Fordringsägare. — Den starkare. —

Leka med elden. — Erik den fjortonde. — Oväder. — Spök-sonaten.) 480 p. 1964.

Queen Christina. Charles XII. Gustav III. (Sw. orig.: Drottning Kristina 1903; Karl XII 1901; Gustav III 1903). Transl. and introduction by W. Johnson. 282 p. Ill. Seattle 1955.

Selected Plays and Prose. Ed. by Robert Brustein. 237 p. New York 1964. (Contains: The Father, Miss Julie, Selections from Inferno, A Dream Play. Sw. orig.: Fadren, Fröken Julie, Inferno, Ett drömspel.)

Seven Plays. The New Definitive Translation by Arvid Paulson. With a General Introduction and Prefaces to the Plays by John Gassner. (Contains: The Father. — Miss Julie. — Comrades. — The Stronger. — The Bond. — Crimes and Crimes. — Easter.) (Sw. orig.: Fadren, Fröken Julie, Kamrater, Den starkare, Bandet, Brott och brott, Påsk.) 342 p. New York 1960.

Six Plays. (Contains: The Father (Fadren 1887); Miss Julie (Fröken Julie 1888); The Stronger (Den starkare 1890); Easter (Påsk 1901); A Dream Play (Ett drömspel 1902); and The Ghost Sonata (Spöksonaten 1907). In new transl. by E. Sprigge. 304 p. Garden City, N. Y. 1955.

Three Plays. The Father. Miss Julie. Easter. Transl. by Peter Watts. (Sw. orig.: Fadren 1887; Fröken Julie 1888; Påsk 1901.) 175 p. Harmondsworth 1958.

Separate Plays:

The Father. A Tragedy in Three Acts. — A Dream Play. Transl. and ed. by Valborg Anderson. (Sw. orig.: Fadren. — Ett dröm-spel.) 138 p. New York 1964.

The Father. Transl. by Edith and Warner Oland. (Sw. orig.: Fadren.) 73 p. Boston 1965.

The Ghost Sonata. (Sw. orig.: Spöksonaten 1907.) Transl. by E. Sprigge. In: Bentley, E. R., The Play. A Critical Anthology. New York 1951.

The Great Highway. A Drama of a Pilgrimage with Seven Road Stops. (Sw. orig.: Stora landsvägen 1909). Transl. by A. Paulson. P. 19—96. In: Modern Scandinavian Plays. New York 1954.

Gustav Adolf. (Sw. orig.: Gustav Adolf 1900.) Transl. and introduction by W. Johnson. 233 p. Ill. Seattle 1957.

Lady Julie. (Sw. orig.: Fröken Julie 1888.) Transl. by C. D. Locock. P. 1—90. In: International Modern Plays. London 1950. The Pelican. (Sw. orig.: Pelikanen 1907.) Transl. by E. Sprinchorn. P. 117—43. In: The Tulane Drama Review. New Orleans: 1960. Playing with Fire. A Play in One Act. Newly transl. by Michael Meyer. (Sw. orig.: Leka med elden 1897.) 35 p. London 1963.

GERMAN:

Hartman, Carl Olov, Prophet und Zimmermann. Spiel in drei Akten. Aus dem Schwedischen übertragen von Ile Meyer-Lüne. Titel der Originalausg.: Profet och timmerman. 39 S. Hamburg 1954.
Johansson, Arthur, Die Attacke. Übertr. von Peter Kleinschmidt. (Originaltitel: Ingen parkett. 1963). Hamburg 1965.
Johansson, Arthur, Dresden. Übertr. von Peter Rienzburg. Hannover 1966.
Johansson, Arthur, Herr Fancy. Übertr. von Klaus-Dieter Schemme. (Originaltitel: Herr Fancy. 1963) Hamburg 1965.
Johansson, Arthur, Die Sitzung geht weiter. Übertr. von Klaus-Dieter Schemme. (Originaltitel: Sammanträde pågår. 1962.) Hamburg 1966.
Johansson, Arthur, Tourist in der Hölle. Übertr. von Klaus-Dieter Schemme. (Originaltitel: Liten mans gunga. 1963) Hamburg 1966.
Johansson, Arthur, Das Ungeheuer. Übertr. Klaus-Dieter Schemme. (Originaltitel: Professorn och monstret. 1965) Hamburg 1966.
Johansson, Arthur, Voll Dampf. Übertr. von Arthur Johansson. (Originaltitel: Full rulle. 1961) Hamburg 1965.
Johansson, Arthur, Der Zinnsoldat. Übertr. von Peter Kleinschmidt. (Originaltitel: Tennsoldaten. 1961) Hamburg 1964.
Moberg, Vilhelm, Lea und Rahel. Ein Frauendrama. Ein Schauspiel in zwei Akten und einem Epilog. Deutsch von Georg Schulte-Frohlinde. (Originaltitel: Lea och Rakel.) 71 S. Hamburg 1956.
Strindberg, August, Werke. München.
Dramen. Neue Übertr. von Willi Reich. 373 S. (1955.)
Dramen. Bd 2. Neue Übertr. von Willi Reich. 322 S. (1957.)

90

Strindberg, August, Dramen. Der Vater, Fräulein Julie, Nach Damaskus, Totentanz, Ein Traumspiel, Gespenstersonate. Neue Übertr. von Willi Reich. (Originaltitel: Fadren, Fröken Julie, Till Damaskus, Dödsdansen, Ett drömspel, Spöksonaten.) 343 S. Hamburg 1960.

Strindberg, August, Dramen. Aus dem Schwedischen von Willi Reich. München & Wien.
Bd. 1. (Der Vater. — Fräulein Julie. — Mutterliebe. — Advent. — Rausch. — Ostern.) 322 S. 1964.
Bd. 2. (Nach Damaskus. — Totentanz.) 361 S. 1964.
Bd. 3. (Die Kronbraut. — Ein Traumspiel. — Unwetter. — Die Brandstätte. — Gespenstersonate. — Der Scheiterhaufen.) 319 S. 1965.

Strindberg, August, Fräulein Julie. Ein naturalistisches Trauerspiel. Neue Übertragung von Willi Reich. 66 S. München 1955.

Strindberg, August, Nach Damaskus. Schauspiel in drei Teilen. Aus dem Schwedischen von Willi Reich. (Originaltitel: Till Damaskus.) 246 S. München 1965.

Strindberg, August, Ostern. Ein Passionsspiel. Aus dem Schwedischen von Willi Reich. Der schwedische Originaltitel lautet: Påsk. 71 S. Stuttgart 1960.

Strindberg, August, Der Scheiterhaufen. Ein Kammerspiel. Mit einer Einführung und Erläuterungen herausg. von Harry Werner. Aus dem Schwedischen von Willi Reich. (Originaltitel: Pelikanen.) 54 S. Paderborn (1964).

Strindberg, August, Totentanz. Aus dem Schwedischen übertr. von Willi Reich. Der schwedische Originaltitel lautet: Dödsdansen. 126 S. Stuttgart 1963.

Strindberg, August, Ein Traumspiel. Deutsch von Peter Weiss. (Originaltitel: Ett drömspel.) 103 S. Frankfurt am Main 1963.

Strindberg, August, Ein Traumspiel. (Drama). Aus dem Schwedischen übers. von Willi Reich. Mit einem Nachwort von Walter A. Berendsohn. Der schwedische Originaltitel lautet: Ett drömspel. 85 S. Stuttgart 1963.

Strindberg, August, Ein Traumspiel. — Die Brandstätte. Mit einem Nachwort von Walter A. Berendsohn. Übers.: Willi Reich. (Originaltitel: Ett drömspel. — Brända tomten.) 141 S. Frankfurt am Main 1963.

Wall, Bengt V., Das Spiel vom Heiligen Menschen. Deutsch von Hannelore Diehl. (Originaltitel: Spelet om den heliga människan.) 75 S. Wien 1967.

Almqvist, C. J. L., Tintomara. Drame en quatre actes et un prologue d'après l'œuvre romanesque de C. J. L. Almqvist "Drottningens Juvelsmycke" (1833). Version scénique et adaptation du suédois de Jacques Robnard. (Multigr.) Paris 1964. 101 p.

Aspenström, Werner, Les enchères. (Auktionen. Dans: Teater 1. 1959.) Trad. et adapt.: Jacques Robnard. (Mimeogr.) Paris 1964. 13 p.

Aspenström, Werner, Party. (Snaskpartyt. Dans: Teater 2. 1963.) Situation tragi-comique en 60 minutes. Trad. et adaptation: Jacques Robnard et Barbro Sundling. (Multigr.) Paris 1963. 25 p.

Bergman, Hjalmar, Une saga. (Sagan. Ecrit en 1919, publ. en 1942.) Pièce en quatre actes. Texte français de Carl-Gustaf Bjurström et Roger Richard. Paris 1959. 32 p.

Bergman, Ingmar, Peinture sur bois. (Trämålning. 1956.) Trad. du suédois par Ulf Ekeram. (Dans: Vingt pièces en un acte, choisies dans le théâtre contemporain. Paris 1959. Pp. 271—287.)

Fahlström, Öyvind, Noël 1965. Les Frères Strindberg et Deux interviews. (Julen 1965. Bröderna Strindberg. Två intervjuer. Dans: Dialog, Stockholm, 1 (1965), No. 1.) Trad. et adapt.: Jacques Robnard. (Multigr.) Paris 1966. 25 p.

Forssell, Lars, Charlie McDeath. (Dans: Forsell, L.: Prototyper. Göteborg 1961. Pp. 33—54.) Trad. et adapt. Jacques Robnard. (Multigr.) Paris 1964. 13 p.

Lagerkvist, Pär, Le tunnel. Pièce en un acte. (Dans: La revue théâtrale, Paris, 7 (1952), No. 21, Pp. 57—67.)

Martinson, Harry, Trois couteaux de Wei. (Tre knivar från Wei. 1964.) Trad. et adapté du suédois par Jacques Robnard. (Multigr.) Paris 1964. 68 p.

Roos, Staffan, Si la guerre éclatait ou un exemple dramatique édifiant. Dans: Young Cinema and Theatre, 4. 1966.

Strindberg, August

Théâtre, Recueils de pièces:

Camarades. (Kamraterna. 1888.) Comédie en cinq actes. Texte français de Maurice Gravier et Georges Rollin. — Paria. (Paria. Dans: Tryckt och otryckt. 1. 1890.) Un acte. Texte français de Michel Arnaud. — Devant la mort. (Inför döden. Dans: Dramatik. 1893). Un acte. Texte français de Tage Aurell. — Il ne faut pas jouer avec le feu. (Leka med elden. Dans: Tryckt och otryckt. 4. 1897.) Comédie en un acte. Texte français de Tore Dahlström et Georges Perros. — Le lien. (Bandet. Ibid.) Tragédie en un acte. Texte français de Tore Dahlström et Jean-Jacques Robert. 1958. 207 p.

L'avent. (Advent. Dans: Vid högre rätt. 1899.) Mystère. Texte français de Tage Aurell et Georges Perros. — Crime et crime. (Brott och brott. Ibid.) Comédie en quatre actes. Texte français de Michèle Cazaux. — Pâques. (Påsk. 1901.) Trois actes. Texte français de C. G. Bjurström et C. A. Ciccione. 1958. 192 p.

Charles XII. (Karl XII. 1901.) Cinq actes. Texte français de Michel Arnaud et C. G. Bjurström. — La reine Christine. (Kristina. Dans: Samlade dramatiska arbeten. 2:2. 1903.) Quatre actes. Texte français de Michèle Cazaux. — Gustave III. (Gustaf III. Ibid.) Quatre actes. Texte français de C. G. Bjurström et Claude Antoine Ciccione. 1960. 222 p.

La danse de mort. (Dödsdansen. 1901.) Edition intégrale. Texte français d'Alfred Jolivet et Georges Perros. 1960. 119 p.

Le songe. (Ett drömspel. Dans: Kronbruden. Svanevit. Drömspelet. 1902.) — Le Hollandais. (Holländarn. Dans: Fagervik och Skamsund. 1902.) — Les babouches d'Abou Kassem. (Abu Casems tofflor. 1908.) — La grand'route. (Stora landsvägen. 1909.) Texte français de Carl-Gustaf Bjurström et André Mathieu. 1960. 237 p.

Orage. (Oväder. 1907.) Texte français de C. G. Bjurström et Georges Perros. — La maison brulée. (Brända tomten. 1907.) Texte français de C. G. Bjurström et Charles Charras. — La sonate des spectres. (Spöksonaten. 1907.) Texte français d'Arthur Adamov et C. G. Bjurström. — Le pélican. (Pelikanen. 1907.) Trois actes. Texte français d'Arthur Adamov. — Le gant noir.

(Svarta handsken. 1909.) Fantaisie poétique (pour la scène) en cinq actes. Texte français de C. G. Bjurström et André Mathieu. — L'île des morts. (Toten-Insel. Dans: Samlade otryckta skrifter. 1. 1918.) Fragment. Texte français de C. G. Bjurström et André Mathieu. 1961. 231 p.

La saga des Folkungar. (Folkungasagan. 1899.) Drame en cinq actes. Texte français de Michel Arnaud et Carl-Gustaf Bjurström. — Gustave Vasa. (Gustaf Vasa. 1899.) Cinq actes. Texte français de Michel Arnaud et Carl-Gustaf Bjurström. 1961. 183 p.

Le voyage de Pierre l'heureux. (Lycko-Pers resa. 1882.) Texte français de Tore Dahlström et André Ortais. — La plus forte. (Den starkare. Dans: Tryckt och otryckt. 2. 1890.) Un acte. Texte français de Tage Aurell et Georges Perros. — Les clefs du ciel. (Himmelrikets nycklar. 1892.) Texte français de Carl-Gustaf Bjurström et André Mathieu. — Premier avertissement. (Första varningen. Dans: Dramatik. 1893.) Un acte. Texte français de Tage Aurell et Georges Perros. — Doit et avoir. (Debet och kredit. Ibid.) Un acte. Texte français de Tage Aurell et Jean-Jacques Robert. — Amour maternel. (Moderskärlek. Ibid.) Un acte. Texte français de Tage Aurell et Georges Perros. 1962. 235 p.

Œuvres dramatiques séparées:

Le chemin de Damas. (Till Damaskus. 1—3. 1—2: 1898. 3: dans Samlade dramatiska arbeten. 1:3. 1904.) Préf. et trad. de A. Jolivet et M. Gravier. Lyon & Paris 1950. 312 p. (Bibl. de la Soc. des Etudes Germaniques. Sér. in-16:3.)

Créanciers. (Fordringsägare. Dans: Tryckt och otryckt. 1. 1890.) Un acte. Texte français d'Alfred Jolivet. Paris 1959. 79 p. (Répertoire pour un théâtre populaire. 19.)

La danse de mort. (Dödsdansen. 1901.) Pièce en deux parties. Trad. dans Théâtre. 4. 1960.

Erik XIV. (Erik XIV. 1899.) Drame en quatre actes. Texte français de Carl-Gustaf Bjurström et Boris Vian. Paris 1958. 78 p. (Répertoire pour un théâtre populaire. 13.)

Le Hollandais. (Holländarn. Dans: Fagervik och Skamsund. 1902.) Un acte. Trad. de Carl-Gustaf Bjurström. (La revue théâtrale, Paris, 9 (1955), pp. 43—47. Aussi dans Théâtre. 5. 1960.

Mademoiselle Julie. (Fröken Julie. 1888.) Un acte. Texte français de Boris Vian. Paris 1957. 80 p. (Répertoire pour un théâtre populaire. 8.)
Autre éd.: Paris 1952. 21 p. (Paris — Théâtre. 66.)
Paria. (Paria. Dans: Tryckt och otryckt. 1. 1890.) Adaptation française de Michel Arnaud. Pièce en un acte. (Dans: L'Avant-scène. Journal du théâtre. No. 127. 1956. Pp. 25—31.)
Autre éd. dans Théâtre. 1. 1958, et dans: Vingt pièces en un acte. Textes choisis et présentés par Odette Aslan. Paris 1959. Pp. 459—476.
Le Pélican. (Pelikanen. 1907.) Trois actes. Texte français d'Arthur Adamov. (Théâtre populaire. Paris. No. 17, mars 1956, pp. 37—62.) Autre éd. dans Théâtre. 6. 1961.
Père. (Fadren. 1887.) Tragédie en trois actes. Trad. d'Arthur Adamov. Paris 1958. 80 p. (Répertoire pour un théâtre populaire. 17.)

BULGARIAN

Strindberg, August, Părvo predureždenie. (Sw. orig.: Första varningen.) Piesa v edno dejstvie. (Prev ot nemski V. Džamdžiev.) P. 287—303. Sofija.
Söderberg, Hjalmar, Ljubov'da e veíčko. Amoromnia. (Gertrud.) Piesa v tri dejstvija. 96 p.Sofija.

CZECH:

Strindberg, August, Nepohrávej s ohněm. (Sw. orig.: Leka med elden.) Veselohra v jednom jednání. Přeložil J. E. Šlechta. 42 p. Praha.
Strindberg, August, Před smrtí. (Sw. orig.: Inför döden.) Truchlohra v jednom jednání. Přeložil J. E. Šlechta. P. 71—92. Praha.
Strindberg, August, Tanec smrti. (Sw. orig.: Dödsdansen.) Přeložil F. V. Krejčí. 1-2. 1. 51 p. 2. 66 p. Kral. Vinohrady.
Wall, Bengt V., Jedna z dvanácti. (De tolv.) Transl. by Karel Tahal. 73 p. Praha 1967.
Wall, Bengt V., O sedmi, kteří nemohli být pověšeni. (Sw. orig.: Historien om de sju som inte kunde hängas.) Přeložil Karel Tahal. 94 p. Praha 1967.

Wall, Bengt V., Hannibal. (Skottet.) Suomen Näyttämöiden Liitto. 58 p. Helsinki 1965.

Wall, Bengt V., Nämä seitsemän, joita ei voitu hirttää. (Historien om de sju som inte kunde hängas.) Suomen Teatteriliitto. 114 p. Helsinki 1967.

Wall, Bengt V., Silentium eli Linnunlaulua ja orgaanista kemiaa. (Silentium eller Fågelsång och organisk kemi.) Suomen Yleisradio. 33 p. Helsinki 1965.

Wall, Bengt V., Väitöskirjamurha. (Avhandlingsmordet.) Suomen Teatteriliitto. 33 p. Helsinki 1966.

ITALIAN:

Teatro svedese. A cura di Clemente Giannini. (Strindberg, August, Danza Macabra (Sw. orig.: Dödsdansen), Pasqua (Sw. orig.: Påsk), Svanevit (Sw. orig.: Svanevit), Un sogno (Sw. orig.: Drömspel), Il Pellicano (Sw. orig.: Pelikanen); Bergman, Hjalmar, La Famiglia Swedenhielm (Sw. orig.: Swedenhielms); Lagerkvist, Pär, Colui che poté rivivere la sua vita (Sw. orig.: Han som fick leva om sitt liv). 511 p. Ill. Milano 1963.

Lagerkvist, Pär, Il carnefice. (Sw. orig.: Bödeln) In: Il dramma. Quindicinale di commedie di grande interesse. P. 9—24. Torino 1952.

Strindberg, August, Il meglio del teatro per la prima volta tradotto dall'originale svedese. (Maestro Olof; Il viaggio di Pietro il fortunato; Il padre; La signorina Giulia; Creditori; Paria; Simum; Il legame; Verso Damasco; Delitto e delitto; Gustavo Vasa; Pasqua; Danza macabra; Il sogno; Tempesta; La casa bruciata; La sonata degli spettri.) Strindberg di Giacomo Oreglia. Strindberg e l'Italia di Torsten Eklund. Strindberg sulle scene del mondo di Gunnar Ollén. 700 p. Torino 1951.

JAPANESE:

Dagerman, Stig, Shikeishū. (Sw. orig.: Den dödsdömde.) P. 319—389. Tōkyō 1953. (In: Gendai sekai gikyoku senshū. 4. Nan-Ō, Hoku-Ō hen.)

Lagerkvist, Pär, Ningen wo iki sasetai. (Sw. orig.: Låt människan leva.) Transl. by Yamamuro Shizuka. P. 297—317. Tōkyō 1953.

(In: Gendai sekai gikyoku senshū. 4. Nan-Ō, Hoku-Ō hen).

Strindberg, August, Fukkatsu-sai hoka. (Sw. orig.: Påsk, Samum, I Rom.) Transl. by Yoshi Ozaki. 149 p. Tōkyō 1954.

Strindberg, August, Yurei sonata. (Sw. orig.: Spöksonaten.) Transl. by Yamamuro Shizuka. P. 171—212. Tōkyō 1953. (In: Gendai sekai gikyoku senshū. 4. Nan-Ō, Hoku-Ō hen.)

POLISH:

Strindberg, August, Dramaty. Mistrz Olof. Ojciec. Panna Julia. Gra snów. Sonata widm. Wybrał i ze szwedzkiego przełożył Zygmunt Łanowski. Tytuły oryginałów: Mäster Olof. Fadren. Fröken Julie. Ett drömspel. Spöksonaten. 436 p. Warszawa 1962.

Strindberg, August, Eryk XIV. Dramat w czterech aktach. Przełożył ze szwedzkiego Zygmunt Łanowski. Tytuł oryginału: Erik XIV. 126 p. Warszawa 1960.

Strindberg, August, Gra snów. (Sw. orig.: Ett drömspel.) Przełożył Zygmunt Łanowski. P. 64—100. Warszawa 1961. (In: Dialog. Rok 6:2.)

RUSSIAN:

Moberg, Vilhelm, Sud'ja. Tragikomedija v šesti dějstvijach. (Sw. orig.: Domaren.) Perevod so švedskogo T. Tumarkinoj. 149 p. Moskva 1960.

Strindberg, August, Tovarišči. Komedija v četerech dějstvijach. (Sw. orig.: Kamraterna.) Perevod so švedskogo L. B. Chavkinoj. 60 p. Moskva.

Söderberg, Hjalmar, Gertruda. Drama v trech dějstvijach. Perevod so švedskogo Ju. Baltrušajtisa. 88 p. Moskva.

SPANISH:

Teatro sueco contemporáneo. Contenido: Pär Lagerkvist, El rey. — Ragnar Josephson, Quizá un poeta. — Stig Dagerman, El condenado a muerte. — Hjalmar Bergman, La familia Sweden-hielm. — Vilhelm Moberg, La mujer del hombre. Traducción del sueco por Javier Armada Abella y Luis Escolar Bareño. Prólogo de Juan Eduardo Zúñiga. 422 p. Ill. Madrid 1960.

Strindberg, August, Los acreedores. Drama en tres cuadros. Versión libre de Alfonso Sastre. (Sw. orig.: Fordringsägare.) 76 p. Madrid 1963. (Colección Teatro. 376.)

Strindberg, *August*, Olof Hoca. (Sw. orig.: Mäster Olof) Bu eseri Mesut Atsiz dilimize çevirmiştir. 160 p. Istanbul 1951.

NOT PRINTED

* = *title not yet translated*

+ = *for information apply to the Swedish Broadcasting Corporation (Sveriges Radio), Box 955, Stockholm 1*

ENGLISH:

Anderberg, *Bengt*, Dante's Inferno. (Sw. orig.: Dantes inferno) Transl. by Leif Sjöberg & Randolph Goodman.

Arnér, *Sivar*, Two (Sw. orig.: Två.) Transl. by Claude Stephenson. 1959.+

Aspenström, *Werner*, The Happy Brothers. (Sw. orig.: De lyckliga bröderna.) Transl. by Paul Britten Austin. 1960.+

Aspenström, *Werner*, The Shadows. (Sw. orig.: Skuggorna.) Transl. by Paul Britten Austin.+

Berglund, *Lars*, Operation Mike. (Sw. orig.: Slaget om Dick) Transl. by Leif Sjöberg & Randolph Goodman.

Berglund, *Lars*, The Tower of Babel. (Sw. orig.: Babels torn.) 1955. Nordiska Teaterförlaget AB.

Bergman, *Ingmar*, The City. (Sw. orig.: Staden.)+

Bergman, *Ingmar*, The Island. (Not yet appeared in Swedish.) Transl. by Paul Britten Austin. 1965.

Bergman, *Ingmar*, Painting on Wood. (Sw. orig.: Trämålning.) Transl. by Paul Britten Austin. BBC.

Bratt, *Bengt*, Grief and Nothing. (Sw. orig.: Sorgen och ingenting.) 1963. Nordiska Teaterförlaget AB.

Bratt, *Bengt*, Night Café. (Sw. orig.: Nattkafé.) Transl. by Claude Stephenson.+

Delblanc, *Sven*, Ariadne and the Peacock. (Sw. orig.: Ariadne och påfågeln.)+

Forssell, *Lars*, Charlie McDeath. (Sw. orig.: Charlie McDeath.) Transl. by Harry G. Carlson. 1963. Nordiska Teaterförlaget AB.

Forssell, *Lars*, The Coronation. (Sw. orig.: Kröningen.) Transl. by Harry G. Carlson. 1962. Nordiska Teaterförlaget AB.

Forssell, Lars, Mary Lou. (Sw. orig.: Mary Lou.) Transl. by Harry G. Carlson. 1960. Nordiska Teaterförlaget AB.

Gierow, Karl Ragnar, By Heart's Delight. (Sw. orig.: Av hjärtans lust.) 1965.⁺

Hergin, Hans, Behold the Hunter's Eye. (Sw. orig.: Si, jägarens öga.) Transl. by Alan Blair. 1960. Folmer Hansens Teaterförlag.

Höijer, Björn-Erik, Beyond the Mountains. (Sw. orig.: Bortom bergen.) Transl. by Elspeth Harley-Schubert. 1963.⁺

Jersild, Per Christian, Notice! Meeting in Progress. (Sw. orig.: Obs! Sammanträde pågår.)⁺

Johansson, Karl Erik, Good Old Pearl. (Sw. orig.: Bara gamla Pärla.) 1967. Folmer Hansens Teaterförlag.

Josephson, Erland, Dear Emanuel and his Antie. (Sw. orig.: Lille Emanuel och hans faster.)⁺

Josephson, Erland, The Parlour Game. (Sw. orig.: Sällskapslek.) Transl. by Birgit Kelsey. 1959. Nordiska Teaterförlaget AB.

Key-Åberg, Sandro, An Empty Room. (Sw. orig.: Ett tomt rum.) Transl. by Rut Link. 1966. Arlecchino Teaterförlag.

Key-Åberg, Sandro, Figures of Speech. (Sw. orig.: Bildade människor.) Transl. by Rut Link. 1966. Arlecchino Teaterförlag.

Key-Åberg, Sandro, Oh. (Sw. orig.: Oh.) Transl. by Brian Rothwell. 1966. Arlecchino Teaterförlag.

Linton-Malmfors, Birgit, The Welcome Home. (Sw. orig.: Välkomstmiddag.) 1962.⁺

Martinson, Harry, Three Knives from Wei. (Sw. orig.: Tre knivar från Wei.) Transl. by Paul Britten Austin. 1967.

Moberg, Vilhelm, Fulfilment. (Sw. orig.: Mans kvinna.) Transl. by M. Heron. 1953. Arlecchino Teaterförlag.

Moberg, Vilhelm, Violation. (Sw. orig.: Våld.) Transl. by Rut Link. 1967. Arlecchino Teaterförlag.

Müller, Erik, Cockfight. (Sw. orig.: Tuppfäktning.) Transl. by L. Holmin. 1960. Nordiska Teaterförlaget AB.

Nordin, Vera, Dance My Doll. (Sw. orig.: Dansa min docka.) 1965. Folmer Hansens Teaterförlag.

Olzon, Staffan, Arthur Fitzgerald in Paris. (Sw. orig.: Arthur Fitzgerald i Paris.)⁺

Runeborg, Björn, Hotel Sydney. (Sw. orig.: Hotel Sydney.) 1966.⁺

Runeborg, Björn, Late Dinner. (Sw. orig.: Utebliven middag.) Transl. by Claude Stephenson. 1965.[+]

Sandgren, Gunnar E, Maranata. (Sw. orig.: I afton bönemöte.) 1967[+]

Schütt, Bertil, Indoor-Game. (Sw. orig.: Inomhuslek.) Transl. by Ida M. Alcock. Nordiska Teaterförlaget AB.

Sjögren, Peder, Encounter in the Park. (Sw. orig.: Möte i parken.)[+]

Sjöman, Vilgot, The Hatbox. (Sw. orig.: Bodil eller hattasken.) 1965. Folmer Hansens Teaterförlag.

Sköld, Bo, My Beloved One Is a Rose. (Sw. orig.: Min kära är en ros.) 1964. Folmer Hansens Teaterförlag.

Strindberg, August, The Pelican. (Sw. orig.: Pelikanen.) Transl. by Paul Britten Austin. BBC.

Werner, Alfred, The Hero. (Sw. orig.: Hjälten.) Transl. by Michael Meyer. 1962. Nordiska Teaterförlaget AB.

Zetterholm, Tore. The Tiger Head. (Sw. orig.: Tigerhuvudet.) 1966. Folmer Hansens Teaterförlag.

Zetterholm, Tore, The Women of Shanghai. (Sw. orig.: Kvinnorna från Shanghai.) 1967. Folmer Hansens Teaterförlag.

GERMAN:

Arnér, Sivar, Allein auf der Landzunge. (Ensam på udden.) Übers. von Tabitha von Bonin.[+]

Arnér, Sivar, Am dritten Tage. (På tredje dagen.) Übers. von Anne Storm. 1961.[+]

Arnér, Sivar, Land in weiter Ferne. (Land långt borta.) Übers. von Tabitha von Bonin.[+]

Arnér, Sivar, Die Sklaven. (Slavarna.) Übers. von Anne Storm. 1965.[+]

Arnér, Sivar, Die Stadt worin wir leben. (Stan vi lever i.) Übers. von Anne Storm. 1966.[+]

Aspenström, Werner, Die glücklichen Brüder. (De lyckliga bröderna.) Übers. von Anton Böhm.[+]

Aspenström, Werner, Das Haus. (Huset.)[+]

Aspenström, Werner, Der Poet und der Kaiser. (Poeten och kejsaren.) 1961.[+]

Aspenström, Werner, The Man Who Didn't Go to the Moon*. (Han som inte for till månen.)[+]

100

Berglund, Lars, Ein Bild aus dem Album. (En bild ur ett album.) 1966.[+]

Bergman, Ingmar, Ein strenger Herr. (Trämålning.) Übers. von Tabitha von Bonin. 1962.[+]

Dagerman, Stig. Der Entdeckungsreisende. (Upptäcktsresanden.) Übers. von Tabitha von Bonin. 1965.[+]

Edwall, Allan, Die Freunde. (Kompisen.) Übers. von Kirsten Hansen-Appel. 1965.[+]

Edwall, Allan, Der Helfer. (Hjälparen.) Übers. von Marianne Weno. 1965.[+]

Evander, Per Gunnar, Es ist Sonntagsnachmittag, da draussen auf dem Feld läuft mein Bruder. (Det är söndagseftermiddag, min bror springer på åkern.) Übers. von Malte Jaeger Hansing.[+]

Forssell, Lars, Die Krönung. (Kröningen.) Übers. von Hannelore Diehl. 1966. Nordiska Teaterförlaget AB.

Forssell, Lars, Der Sonntagsspaziergang. (Söndagspromenaden.) Übers. von Hannelore Diehl. 1966. Nordiska Teaterförlaget AB.

Forssell, Lars, Der Starrkopf. (Galenpannan.) Übers. von Hannelore Diehl. 1966. Nordiska Teaterförlaget AB.

Grevenius, Herbert, The Girl from Afar.* (Flickan från fjärran.)[+]

Grevenius, Herbert, Ordinary People*. (Som folk är mest.)[+]

Grevenius, Herbert, Train 56*. (Tåg 56.)

Gustafsson, Bosse, Audienz. (Audiens.) Übers. von Adolf Schütz.[+]

Hergin, Hans, Eine Blume für Ida. (En blomma till Ida.) Übers. von Tabitha von Bonin.[+]

Hergin, Hans, After the Last Train.* (Efter sista tåget.) Übers. von Tabitha von Bonin.[+]

Hergin, Hans, Linus unter Licht der Sterne. (Linus under stjärnors ljus.) Übers. von Thyra Dohrenburg.[+]

Hergin, Hans, Ruf in die Nacht. (Du ropar i natten.)[+]

Hergin, Hans, Seh, das Auge des Jägers. (Si, jägarens öga.) Übers. von Thyra Dohrenburg.[+]

Husahr, Owe, Ein Strom von Zeit. (Sommarbalkong.) Übers. von Tabitha von Bonin.[+]

Höijer, Björn-Erik, Arons Stab. (Arons stav.) Übers. von Anton Böhm.[+]

Höijer, Björn-Erik, Königin der Nacht. (Nattens drottning.) Übers. von Tabitha von Bonin.[+]

Höijer, Björn-Erik, Und ob Du dichten kannst, Kristoffer. (Visst kan du dikta, Kristoffer.) Übers. von Anton Böhm.[+]

Johansson, Karl Erik Good Old Pearl.* (Bara gamla Pärla.) Folmer Hansens Teaterförlag.

Josephson, Erland, Gesellschaftsspiel. (Sällskapslek.) Übers. von Adolf Schütz. 1956. Nordiska Teaterförlaget AB.

Josephson, Erland, König ausser Dienst. (Kungen ur leken.) Übers. von Dorothea Bjelfvenstam. 1960. Nordiska Teaterförlaget AB.

Josephson, Erland, Die schöne Hélène. (Den sköna Helena.) Übers. von Malte Jaeger Hansing.[+]

Josephson, Erland, Wenn wir spielen. (Om vi leker.)[+]

Key-Åberg, Sandro, Oh. (Oh.) 1966. Arlecchino Teaterförlag.

Laestadius, Lars Levi, Mr. Brisk Breaks All Bounds.* (Herr Blink går över alla gränser.)[+]

Lidman, Sara, Hiob Uhrmachers Tochter. (Job Klockmakares dotter.) Übers. von Born-Pilsach. 1956. Nordiska Teaterförlaget AB.

Löttiger, Olof, Das Schloss über dem Dorf. (Slottet vid byn.) Übers. von Malte Jaeger Hansing.[+]

Moberg, Vilhelm, Am Abend vor dem Markt. (Marknadsafton.) Übers. von Kirsten Hansen-Appel. 1967. Arlecchino Teaterförlag.

Moberg, Vilhelm, Das Defizit. (Kassabrist.) 1966. Arlecchino Teaterförlag.

Moberg, Vilhelm, Die geballten Hände. (De knutna händerna.) 1966. Arlecchino Teaterförlag.

Moberg, Vilhelm, Jarl der Witwer. (Änkeman Jarl.) Übers. von Kirsten Hansen-Appel. 1967. Arlecchino Teaterförlag.

Moberg, Vilhelm, Lea und Rahel. (Lea och Rakel.) Übers. von Georg Schulte-Frohlinde. 1956. Arlecchino Teaterförlag.

Moberg, Vilhelm, Das Mädchenzimmer. (Jungfrukammare.) 1966. Arlecchino Teaterförlag.

Moberg, Vilhelm, Der Nachtkellner. (Nattkyparen.) Übers. von Franz Schafranek. 1967. Arlecchino Teaterförlag.

Moberg, Vilhelm, Der Richter. (Domaren.) 1966. Arlecchino Teaterförlag.

Müller, Erik, Drei Kreise. (Tre cirklar.) Übers. von Hans Verder. 1950. Nordiska Teaterförlaget AB.

Müller, Erik, Die Mutter. (Modern.)[+]

Orre, Ingvar, Nacht mit Zahnschmerzen. (Natt med tandvärk.) Übers. von Kirsten Hansen-Appel.[+]

Orre, Ingvar, Broken Clock.* (Sönderslagen klocka.)[+]

Oxelqvist, Rune, Der Prügelknabe. (Hackkycklingen.)[+]

Runeborg, Björn, Hotel Sidney. (Hotel Sydney.)[+]

Runeborg, Björn, Late Dinner.* (Utebliven middag.)[+]

Siwertz, Sigfrid, Djami and the Water Sprites*. (Djami och vattenandarna.)[+]

Sjögren, Peder, Begegnung im Park. (Möte i parken.) Übers. von Kirsten Hansen-Appel. 1963.[+]

Sjöman, Vilgot, Bodil. (Bodil eller hattasken.) Übers. von Paul Patera. 1967. Folmer Hansens Teaterförlag.

Sköld, Bo, Meine Liebste ist eine Rose. (Min kära är en ros.) 1962. Folmer Hansens Teaterförlag.

Strindberg, August, The Débutante.* An episode from "The Red Room" (Debutanten. Episod ur Strindbergs Röda rummet.) Übers. von Tabitha von Bonin.[+]

Wall, Bengt V., Die Geschichte von den sieben die man nicht hängen konnte. (Historien om de sju som inte kunde hängas.) Übers. von Erika Richter. 1964. Nordiska Teaterförlaget AB.

Wall, Bengt V., Die Komödie des Autoren. (Författarens komedi.) Übers. von Erika Richter. 1964. Nordiska Teaterförlaget AB.

Wall, Bengt V., Silentium oder Vogelgesang und organische Chemie. Deutsch von Erika Richter. (Silentium eller Fågelsång och organisk kemi.) 1965.

Werner, Alfred, Theseus. (Hjälten.) Übers. von Inge Waern. 1961. Nordiska Teaterförlaget AB.

Zetterholm, Tore, Der brennende Speer. (Det brinnande spjutet.) Folmer Hansens Teaterförlag.

Zetterholm, Tore, Der Flohmarkt. (Loppmarknad.) Folmer Hansens Teaterförlag.

Zetterholm, Tore, The Women of Shanghai*. (Kvinnorna från Shanghai.) 1967. Folmer Hansens Teaterförlag.

Zetterholm, Tore, Modell Beatrice. (Modell Beatrice.) Folmer Hansens Teaterförlag.

Zetterholm, Tore, Und sie beteten den Drachen an. (Vilddjurets bild.) Folmer Hansens Teaterförlag.

Zetterholm, Tore, Wer war Ellen Miller? (Ingen mans land.) Folmer Hansens Teaterförlag.

FRENCH:

Arnér, Sivar, Deux. (Två.) Trad. par Jacques Gengoux. 1959.+

Arnér, Sivar, Un très lointain pays. (Land långt borta.) Trad. par Aimé Sakari et Roger Richard. 1953.+

Aspenström, Werner, L'empereur et le poète. (Poeten och kejsaren.) Paris 1960.

Aspenström, Werner, Les évasions illusoires. (En clown måste ha gått vilse.) Trad. par Carole Blanc-Paulsen.+

Aspenström, Werner, Les Frères Heureux. (De lyckliga bröderna.) Adaptation Jacques Robnard. Paris 1962.

Aspenström, Werner, Les ombres. (Skuggorna.) Adaptation Jacques Robnard. Paris 1962.

Bergman, Ingmar, Le cité. (Staden.)+

Bratt, Bengt, Café de nuit. (Nattkafé.) Trad. par Roger Girod et Michel Hallard.+

Fahlström, Öyvind, Oswald revient. En cours de traduction, Jacques Robnard, Paris.

Forssell, Lars, Charlie McDeath. (Charlie McDeath.) Trad. par Jacques Robnard. 1965. Nordiska Teaterförlaget AB.

Hergin, Hans, Un cyclamen pour Ida. (En blomma till Ida.) Trad. par Carole Blanc-Paulsen. 1960. Folmer Hansens Teaterförlag.

Höijer, Björn-Erik, Au delà des monts. (Bortom bergen.)+

Josephson, Erland, Benjamin. (Benjamin.) Adaptation française: Jacques Robnard. Paris 1961.

Key-Åberg, Sandro, "Oh!", bla-bla-blas. (Oh.) Adaptation Jacques Robnard. Paris 1967.

Klintberg, Bengt af, Lidner. (Lidner.) Trad. par Jacques Robnard. 1966. Arlecchino Teaterförlag.

Linton-Malmfors, Birgit, On fête un retour. (Välkomstmiddag.)+

Olzon, Staffan, Arthur Fitzgerald à Paris. (Arthur Fitzgerald i Paris.)[+]

Runeborg, Björn, Dîner remis. (Utebliven middag.) Trad. par Malou Höijer.[+]

Runeborg, Björn, L'Hôtel Sydney. (Hotel Sydney.)[+]

Schütt, Bertil, La Femme Cheval. (Inomhuslek.) Adaptation Maurice Gravier. 1966. Nordiska Teaterförlaget AB.

Sjögren, Peder, Rencontre dans un Parc. (Möte i parken.) 1962.[+]

Strindberg, Axel, Le fils de calif. (Kalifens son.) Trad. par Olivier Maurice. 1950. Nordiska Teaterförlaget AB.

Taube, Evert, Richard Cœur de Lion et Philippe II. (Rickard Lejonhjärta och Filip II.) Trad. par Malou Höijer. 1967. Arlecchino Teaterförlag.

BULGARIAN:

Arnér, Sivar, The Slaves*. (Slavarna.) 1967.[+]

CZECH:

Runeborg, Björn, Hotel Sydney.[+]

Wall, Bengt V., As Long as the Bird Is Singing*. (Så länge fågeln sjunger.) 1967.

Wall, Bengt V., The Deserter*. (Desertören.) 1967/68.

Wall, Bengt V., The Play About the Holy Man*. (Spelet om den heliga människan.) 1967/68.

Wall, Bengt V., The Thesis Murder,* (Avhandlingsmordet.) 1966.

DUTCH:

Hergin, Hans, Een bloemetje voor Ida. (En blomma till Ida.) Transl. by Mirja Novalainen.[+]

FINNISH:

Ardelius, Lars, Luonnonlaulaja. (Natursångaren.)[+]

Arnér, Sivar, Etäinen maa. (Land långt borta.) 1960.[+]

Arnér, Sivar, Two*. (Två.) 1960.[+]

Aspenström, Werner, Näyttelijän kuolema. (En skådespelares död.)[+]

Aspenström, Werner, Runoilija ja keisari. (Poeten och kejsaren.)[+]

Berglund, Lars, Cyranon muotokuva. (Porträtt av Cyrano.)[+]

Berglund, Lars, Hattuliike Mia. (Ateljé Mia.)+
Berglund, Lars, Mitalin toinen puoli. (Medaljens baksida.)+
Bergman, Hjalmar, Hänen armonsa testamentti. (Hans nåds testamente.)+
Bergman, Hjalmar, Herra Sleeman tulee. (Herr Sleeman kommer.)+
Bergman, Hjalmar, Isoäiti ja Hyvä Jumala. (Farmor och Vår Herre.)+
Bergman, Hjalmar, Jäähyväiset. (Avsked.)+
Bergman, Hjalmar, Swedenhjelmit. (Swedenhielms.)+
Bergman, Hjalmar, Tanssi. (Dans.)+
Bergman, Ingmar, Puumaalaus. (Trämålning.)+
Björkman, Lars, Joulu loistolähiössä. (Jul i trivselmyra.)+
Boye, Karin, Temppelin kannattaja. (Hon som bär templet.)+
Brenner, Arvid, Sunnuntaitutkisteluja. (Betraktelsen.)+
Dagerman, Stig, Pikku kesämme. (Vår lilla sommar.)+
Edwall, Allan, Kaveri. (Kompisen.)+
Grevenius, Herbert, Huone ja keittokomero. (Rum med kokvrå.)+
Grevenius, Herbert, Ja koko konttori kohisi. (Storm på kontor.)+
Grevenius, Herbert, Juna 56. (Tåg 56.)+
Grevenius, Herbert, Me kolme uutta. (Vi tre debuterar.)+
Grevenius, Herbert, Ordinary People*. (Som folk är mest.)+
Grevenius, Herbert, Vieras veräjällä. (Främling vid grinden.)+
Grevenius, Herbert, Viimeinen laituri. (Sista bryggan.)+
Henriksson, Alf, Kivenmurskausmoraliteetti. (Moralitet vid en stenkross.)+
Hergin, Hans, After the Last Train.* (Efter sista tåget.)+
Hergin, Hans, Kukka Idalle. (En blomma till Ida.) Transl. by Urpo Lauri.+
Höijer, Björn-Erik, Onni ajaa autolla. (Monica.)+
Höijer, Björn-Erik, Seitsemän joulukynttilää. (Sju ljus till änkefru Karlsson.)+
Höijer, Björn-Erik, Tuvan täydeltä lämmintä. (En sorts nödvändighet.)+
Höijer, Björn Erik, Vuoren tuolla puolen. (Bortom bergen.)+
Johnson, Eyvind, Kaupunki pimeässä. (Stad i mörker.)+
Josephson, Erland, Tämä meidän puistomme. (Vår egen park.)+
Lagerkvist, Pär, Antakaa ihmisen elää. (Låt människan leva.)+
Lagerkvist, Pär, Pyöveli. (Bödeln.)+

Lind, Pi, Modernin ihmisen mahdollisuudet sielullisiin kokemuksiin tekniikan aikakautena. (Den moderna människans möjligheter till själsliga upplevelser i en teknisk tid.)[+]

Lindsjö, Inga, Pikkuäti. (Morsan.) 1963. Nordiska Teaterförlaget AB

Linton, Irène, Majakkasaaren opettajatar. (Fyrlärarinnan.)[+]

Löttiger, Olof, Sininen arki. (Blå vardag.)[+]

Martinson, Harry, Molukkien luotsi. (Lotsen från Moluckas.)[+]

Moberg, Vilhelm, Kassavaillinki. (Kassabrist.)[+]

Moberg, Vilhelm, Lea ja Raakel. (Lea och Rakel.)[+]

Moberg, Vilhelm, Leskimies Jarl. (Änkeman Jarl.)[+]

Moberg, Vilhelm, Markkinoille lähtö. (Marknadsafton.)[+]

Moberg, Vilhelm, Sata kertaa naimisissa. (Hundra gånger gifta.)[+]

Müller, Erik, Neitsytkammio. (Jungfruburen.)[+]

Orre, Ingvar, Jono. (Kö.)[+]

Orre, Ingvar, Rikottu kello. (Sönderslagen klocka.)[+]

Perrolf, Bertil, Kielletty ovi. (Förbjuden utgång.)[+]

Rosendahl, Sven, Pois noidankehästä. (Svart vår.)[+]

Runeborg, Björn, Hotelli Sidney. (Hotel Sydney.)[+]

Runeborg, Björn, Mies josta tuli kaupunki. (Mannen som blev en stad.)[+]

Runeborg, Björn, Myöhästynyt päivällinen. (Utebliven middag.)[+]

Runeborg, Björn, Piazzalla. (På piazzan.)[+]

Sandgren, Gustav, Ohikulkija vain. (Den förlorade sonen.)[+]

Sandgren, Gustav, Taloudenhoitaja tositarkoituksella. (Bröderna Lind.)[+]

Schütt, Bertil, Fredrik käärmeenkolossa. (Fredrik i ormgropen.)[+]

Siwertz, Sigfrid, Renessanssisänky. (Renässanssängen.)[+]

Sjögren, Peder, Kohtaus puistossa. (Möte i parken.)[+]

Sjöstrand, Östen, Paimenet ja kuninkaat. (Ett julspel.)[+]

Stolpe, Sven, Kastikekulho. (Såsskålen.)[+]

Söderberg, Hjalmar, Totinen leikki. (Den allvarsamma leken.)[+]

Wall, Bengt V., The Thesis Murder.* (Avhandlingsmordet.)

Widding, Lars, Rastas. (Trasten.)[+]

Värnlund, Rudolf, U 39. (U 39.)[+]

Zetterholm, Tore, Tiikeri-Harry. (Tiger-Harry.)

Zetterholm, Tore, The Image of the Beast*. (Vilddjurets bild.)[+]

HUNGARIAN:

Arnér, Sivar, Magány. (Alla de andra.) Transl. by Birkás Endre. 1966.[+]

Runeborg, Björn, Hotel Sydney.[+]

ITALIAN:

Arnér, Sivar, Land Far Away*. (Land långt borta.)[+]
Müller, Erik, Furia d'Amore. (Modern.)[+]
Müller, Erik, Cross the Street*. (Gå över gatan.)[+]
Runeborg, Björn, Hotel Sydney.[+]
Runeborg, Björn, Late Dinner*. (Utebliven middag.)[+]
Sjögren, Peder, Rincontro nel Parco. (Möte i parken.)[+]

POLISH:

Anderberg, Bengt, Piekło Dantego. (Dantes Inferno.) Transl. by Zygmunt Łanowski. 1964.

Moberg, Vilhelm, Żona. (Hustrun.) Transl. by Zygmunt Łanowski. 1957.

Strindberg, August, Burza. (Oväder.) Transl. by Zygmunt Łanowski. 1967.

Strindberg, August, Pelikan. (Pelikanen.) Transl. by Zygmunt Łanowski. 1965.

Strindberg, August, Śmiertelny taniec. (Dödsdansen.) Gdańsk. 1967.

PORTUGUESE:

Strindberg, August, A mais forte. (Den starkare.) Transl. by Knut Bernström. 1957.

Strindberg, August, A Senhorita Júlia. (Fröken Julie.) Transl. by Knut Bernström. 1958.

ROUMANIAN:

Wall, Bengt V., Povestea celor şapte ce n-au putut fi spînzuraţi (Sw. orig.: Historien om de sju som inte kunde hängas.) Centrul de documentare teatrală şi muzicală. Bucureşti 1967.

RUSSIAN:

Hergin, Hans, A Flower for Ida.* (En blomma till Ida.)[+]

SERBO-CROATIAN:

Höijer, Björn-Erik, One Day*. (En dag.)[+]

SPANISH:

Moberg, Vilhelm, La Mujer del hombre. (Mans kvinna.) Transl. by Javier Armada Abella. 1967. Arlecchino Teaterförlag.

Strindberg, August, La Señorita Julia. (Fröken Julie.) Transl. by Knut Bernström. 1965.

PHOTOGRAPHERS

Ove Alström p. 13, 19, 49, 72, 73
Beata Bergström p. 26, 30, 33, 37, 38, 39, 41, 45, 61, 63
Werner Goldbach p. 69, 71
Lennart Jansson p. 82
Bruno Müller p. 47
Sven-Åke Persson p. 83
Sallstedts Bildbyrå p. 20, 77, 79
Skåne-Reportage p. 43, 81
Studio Järlås p. 32
Uppsala-Bild p. 17